Uncovering Online Commenting Culture

Renee Barnes

Uncovering Online
Commenting Culture

Trolls, Fanboys and Lurkers

Renee Barnes
Faculty of Arts, Business and Law
University of the Sunshine Coast
Sippy Downs, QLD, Australia

ISBN 978-3-319-70234-6   ISBN 978-3-319-70235-3   (eBook)
https://doi.org/10.1007/978-3-319-70235-3

Library of Congress Control Number: 2017960845

Cover illustration: Détail de la Tour Eiffel © nemesis2207/Fotolia.co.uk

Printed on acid-free paper

This Palgrave Macmillan imprint is published by Springer Nature
The registered company is Springer International Publishing AG
The registered company address is: Gewerbestrasse 11, 6330 Cham, Switzerland

For B., C. and D.

PREFACE

As a journalism academic my interest in commenting began in the early 2000s with a focus on the comments following news stories. At this time, most research was focused on the impact of the inclusion of these comments on the news production process and the role of journalists in managing these comments. I, however, was (and still am) interested in the people who were making these comments. Who were they? What motivated them to leave a comment? What type of comments did they leave and why did they leave those particular comments?

Inevitably when discussing my work with family and friends the response would generally be something along the lines of: "Comments are terrible! They are full of rubbish. You won't get any sense there." Many would claim to never read the comments, let alone make a comment (despite research and analytics at the time showing comment threads were highly read). This disconnect between what appeared to be happening in these comment threads and the perception of what was happening there fascinated me.

Fast-forward to now, 2017, and my interest in commenting is not restricted to those following news stories, but to all of the platforms that facilitate interaction and discussion through commenting: social media, participatory websites, and forums. Despite the many multimedia methods of communication that the internet offers, text-based communication, or commenting, still remains the most prevalent.

Given that our offline life bleeds into our online life, and vice versa, we must have an understanding of the dynamics that are at play in these interactions. We socialise, meet our partners and work in interactive online spaces—they are a fundamental part of our life. While the internet has brought these new means of communication and interactivity, it is often the darker side of communication—incivility, abuse and harassment—that is synonymous with this new frontier. Yet despite our general unease with this aspect of online interaction, there still seems to be a disconnect, however a far more disturbing one. Too often when we discuss the issues of online abuse, we shake our heads, shrug our shoulders and assume there is nothing we can do. Again, when discussing my work, and in particular the often hostile nature of comments, I am often confronted with: "Well it's the internet—what do you expect?" I believe we can and should expect more.

The aspects of our life that will be played out online will only increase and the costs of online abuse are real—they have serious social and economic consequences. So, at the heart of this book is the question: "How can we create harmonious and inclusive communities online?"

To address this question I draw a more comprehensive model for understanding the contributing factors to commenting culture by drawing from media and cultural studies, sociology and psychology. To begin, I outline the landscape of the online domain in which we make comments. By reviewing the current research on the online community I argue that a broader, more encompassing, approach is needed. Specifically, I situate our online interactions within an online community. This is an important distinction. If we are to expect the same of those we associate with online as we do offline, then considering these interactions as taking place within a community is vital. This will ensure that we postion online abuse and other anti-social behaviours as broader social problems, rather than internet problems.

Next, I will draw on the rich field of fan studies to examine the fundamental role that emotion and affect plays in guiding our commenting behaviour. Understanding the role that emotion plays in our engagement provides an important pillar in participatory culture. Fan studies also helps provide new subjectivities, the anti-fan and non-fan as frameworks for understanding why we behave the way we do when commenting online.

Media is then viewed through the lens of practice theory to determine how our media usage orders, controls and anchors other social and cultural practices and vice versa. I then look to personality, specifically the Big Five Inventory, to examine how individual difference influences commenting behaviour. By understanding the role of personality in commenting behaviour, we can also draw conclusions about the technological affordances of commenting platforms that encourage pro-social behaviour

Finally, I draw on the gaming industry, as a case, to examine the role that the institutions operating the spaces in which we comment have in regulating behaviour and forming community expectations.

Used together, these approaches enable a comprehensive understanding of commenting culture; how we, as individuals and collectively, can influence the online communities in which we engage; and the role that the institutions play in creating harmonious and inclusive online spaces. Taken together, the work surveyed provides a participatory model for understanding commenting culture.

I hope that the participatory model outlined in this book can be used to adjust our expectations of the online domain to mimic the expectations we have of "real life". The model is also aimed at informing the education of individuals and institutions, helping them understand how they can influence commenting culture. It is also hoped it will provide a framework for media scholars to more thoroughly interrogate online commenting practice.

Sippy Downs, QLD, Australia   Renee Barnes

ACKNOWLEDGMENTS

This work has emerged from various projects and collaborations. In particular, the chapter that addresses personality would not have been possible without the wisdom and guidance of Professor Doug Mahar. Doug introduced me to the study of personality through our project: Personality and Online News Commenters. It was through this project (funded by internal grants at the University of the Sunshine Coast) that I began to understand the role of individual difference in commenting behaviours. I am also greatly indebted to the research assistants who provided literature research and support on that project: Ides Wong and Karina Rune. I also thank Professor Sue Turnbull, for introducing me to the world of fan studies and her continued mentoring and support. I also want to thank my close colleagues at the University of the Sunshine Coast, Jane Fynes Clinton and Peter English. They both provided invaluable support throughout the process of researching and writing this book. Peter also provided invaluable feedback on earlier drafts. I also wish to thank the reviewers of this manuscript. They provided constructive advice that has greatly improved the final product. Finally, a special thanks to Madison Hadland who crafted the diagram of the participatory model in Chap. 6.

Contents

1 Hitch Up the Wagon: Charting the Online Commenting
   Landscape   1

2 You Either Love It or You Hate It! The Emotional
   and Affective Factors of Commenting   27

3 The Online/Offline Life   47

4 A Neurotic Extravert with a Pinch of Conscientiousness?
   How Personality Informs Commenting Behaviours   67

5 Lessons from #*Gamergate*   93

6 Conclusion: A Participatory Model for Understanding
   Commenting Culture   113

Index   129

LIST OF TABLES

Table 4.1   Personality traits and online activity   79
Table 5.1   *League of Legends* responses to toxic gaming behaviour   96

CHAPTER 1

Hitch Up the Wagon: Charting the Online Commenting Landscape

In the American pioneering era, settlers hitched up wagons to conquer what they saw as the vast, lawless and untamed areas west of the Mississippi River. As the white settlers moved in, they established new communities and sought their fortunes. This picture of the "Wild West" depicted in popular culture is often used as an analogy for the digital landscape in which we carry out our personal and professional relationships. Indeed, Howard Rheingold's (2000) seminal book *Virtual Communities: Homesteading on the Electronic Frontier* invokes this imagery.

Typically, the analogy is used to correlate the lawlessness associated with the gunslingers of the Wild West with the anti-social behaviours that concern us most in our online interactions: incivility, hostility, "trolling", online harassment and abuse. Increasingly it is these aspects of the internet which are causing us the most unease and concern. Of course, uncivil and hostile behaviour is not unique to the online space, but the persistent and ubiquitous nature of online communications enhances the social implications of these anti-social behaviours.

In seeking to address the question "How can we create harmonious and inclusive communities online?", we must first chart the landscape in which we are commenting to determine what can be adjusted and influenced. This chapter sets out to chart the Wild West of the online commenting landscape by defining the platforms where we comment and exploring how and why we comment. Next, it will draw on the concept of the online community to investigate the unique circumstances that influence our relationships online and the social implications of those

© The Author(s) 2018
R. Barnes, *Uncovering Online Commenting Culture*,
https://doi.org/10.1007/978-3-319-70235-3_1

1

relationships—in other words, how people behave online and how that behaviour impacts on others. The use of the online community is a central pillar to the argument outlined in this book, as understanding our online interactions as taking part in a community is vital if we are to adjust our expectations of acceptable behaviours online.

The chapter will conclude by outlining the factors that influence how we as individuals and collectively can affect the climate of the online domain and the role the institutions that own the online commenting platforms have in forming normative online behaviours through their policies and technological interventions. Overall, an examination of the research available on online commenting finds it either focuses solely on defining our online behaviours or takes a narrow approach to examining motivations behind this behaviour. Instead it will be argued here that a more holistic approach, which considers the myriad of factors that contribute to the type and quality of online interaction, must be used if we are truly going to understand online commenting behaviour.

Mapping the Boundaries

Just as intense attention was paid to establishing the boundaries of emerging territories in the pioneering era, much attention has been paid to defining the various platforms on which we encounter each other online. The terms used to describe social media or social networking sites, in particular, have been contentious.

boyd and Ellison (2007, p. 11) argue we should refer to these platforms as "social network sites" as opposed to "social networking sites" because

> [n]etworking emphasizes relationship initiation, often between strangers. While networking is possible on these sites, it is not the primary practice on many of them, nor is it what differentiates them from other forms of computer-mediated communication (CMC).

However, this specificity has been criticised because it is, in fact, too broad: "given these rapid cultural shifts and the dynamic and disjointed nature of much contemporary online culture there is a pressing *need to classify* in order to work toward a more descriptive analysis" (Beer 2008, p. 518; emphasis in original). Despite this, "social networking sites", "social network sites" and "social media" tend to be used interchangeably in the literature.

Kaplan and Haenlein (2010, p. 61) use the term "social media" and define it as a group of internet based applications that evolved from Web 2.0, "a platform whereby content and applications are continuously modified by all users in a participatory and collaborative fashion". The term "social media" can be further parsed into collaborative projects, blogs, content communities and virtual worlds. Collaborative projects involve the joint and simultaneous creation of content by many end-users and include sites such as Wikipedia (Kaplan and Haenlein 2010). Blogs are usually managed by one person only, but are conversational and collaborative and provide the possibility of interaction with others through the addition of comments (Lowrey 2006; Kaplan and Haenlein 2010). Content communities exist to share content between users and include sites such as Flickr and YouTube (Kaplan and Haenlein 2010; Barker et al. 2015). These sites facilitate commentary in response to the content posted. Finally, virtual worlds are platforms that replicate the "real" world, allowing users to appear as personalised avatars and interact with each other. They come in the form of games (for example, *World of Warcraft*) or social worlds such as *Second Life* (Kaplan and Haenlein 2010).

This book is concerned with comments, as they remain the primary method in which we engage with and react to each other in the online space. It is therefore focused on the spaces that facilitate the making of comments. These include social networking sites, collaborative projects, blogs and content communities, as outlined above. They also include other participatory websites that enable commenting, such as specialist forums (for example, Lonely Planet's Thorn Tree travel forum), e-commerce sites (for example, Amazon), news websites and user-review sites (for example, TripAdvisor).

Defining the platforms where we interact via comments is important as different environments will offer different controls on sociality. The space in which we comment is one of the many factors that influence our commenting behaviour. So, if we first understand where it is that we are commenting, then we can determine what measures can be taken to enhance or alter commenting behaviour.

Understanding Online Discussion

Within these spaces, previous research has focused on comments as a vehicle that enables deliberation and interaction. Deliberation occurs when people "engage in reasoned opinion expression on a social or political issue in an attempt to identify solutions to a common problem and to evaluate those solutions" (Habermas 1984). Elements of deliberation are most likely to occur in our everyday discussions with individuals whose views differ from our own (see Hutchens et al. 2015). Deliberation is enabled by both the observation of a debate (comment reading) and engagement with a debate (commenting) (Springer et al. 2015).

While all of the outlined platforms are participatory environments that enable deliberation through comments, how we build relationships on them and therefore how we comment does differ from individual to individual. Springer et al. (2015) have argued that people who comment either do so in a unidirectional fashion, to publish their own opinions, or in an interpersonal fashion, to react to other commenters. This interpersonal communication may be either consensual communication, wherein commenters want to express their agreement, or confrontational or discursive communication, wherein they do not agree and want to express criticism. The latter evokes debates (Wojcieszak and Mutz 2009).

Many scholars argue that online deliberation can ensure access to a more diverse range of people and opinions (see Heatherly et al. 2016), as hearing the other side of an argument has been considered a necessary precondition for the beneficial effects of deliberative discussion (Carpini et al. 2004).

This broadening of informational access is discussed in terms of "cross-cutting discussion", which refers to exchanges of ideas among people who hold differing political and ideological beliefs. It has been argued that cross-cutting discussions encourage greater interpersonal deliberation and more tolerance of others and are therefore fundamental for deliberative democracy (Mutz 2006). Twitter hashtags have been shown to facilitate cross-cutting discussion as they enable communities that hold opposing views to have greater contact (Conover et al. 2012). An individual's endorsement of a news story through a Facebook "like" ("Like") has also been shown to increase exposure to news from politically diverse sources for partisans and non-partisans alike (Messing and Westwood 2012). However, an awareness of other people's political opinions through online discussion could inspire a "spiral of silence", whereby an individual will self-censor if he or she does not share the opinions of those in his or her network (Scheufle and Moy 2000). In this instance exposure to cross-cutting discussion may mean exposure to more diverse views, but it will result in less robust debate, as many people may choose to remain silent. Incivility by people with contrary or opposing views has also been shown to have a negative impact on cross-cutting discussion, as individuals subjected to this type of behaviour are more likely to become close minded and give uncivil responses (Hwang et al. 2016).

Other scholars however, argue that, while there may be increasing opportunities to access a broader range of information online, we choose to filter this information down to that which reflects our existing attitudes and opinions (Knobloch-Westerwick and Johnson 2014; Knobloch-Westerwick and Meng 2011; Stroud 2010). This filtering may take place either through our selections of participatory websites to visit (for example, a particular news website) or by managing our networks so that we are not exposed to contrary views. The choice of a website (generally one providing political information) is made giving consideration to the possibility of finding content that reinforces our existing opinions (Holbert et al. 2010; Heatherly et al. 2016), but is also based on the perceived audience of that participatory space (Dvir Gvirsman 2016). Dvir Gvirsman (2016) argues that the contemporary online environment promotes "audience homophily", where media consumers favour certain websites not only due to their content but also due to their audience. Our preference for partisan media websites catering to a homogeneous, likeminded consumership is explained in terms of the need for self-consistency. Over time, this behaviour will polarise an individual's political identity through a spiral of reinforcement. Furthermore, individuals with more extreme ideologies will present higher levels of audience homophily and, over time, that audience homophily will be associated with ideological polarisation, intolerance and political self-definition. This suggests, then, that some of the more anti-social online behaviours related to intolerance could increase over time, so that the online commenting environment may increase in its hostility and incivility because of this spiral of reinforcement. This is obviously cause for great concern when we consider some of the more troubling online behaviours, which will be discussed later.

Of course, not all discussion that takes place online is related to politics, and for some people it is a deliberate choice to filter out political discussion. Instead, commenting online is a simple form of interaction that can contribute to the "creation" of self. Livingstone (2008) argues that social media in particular has become a space for the cultivation and management of identity. While Raine and Smith (2012) found that a significant number of social media users block, hide or unfriend individuals who post political views contrary to their own or who post too often about politics. In this way individuals are filtering discussion by adapting and managing their network.

Therefore, we have opportunities online to both broaden and narrow our access to a diverse range of people and opinions. Whether we join cross-cutting discussions or filter out opposing views depends on which platforms we access and the networks we establish.

Drawing on the theoretical approach of uses and gratifications, other studies have sought to examine how we interact online by focusing on what motivates us to leave a comment. Overall, we are motivated by individual-centric reasons (informational, personal-identity and entertainment motives) and social interaction. Informational motives are behind comments left by people as a means of educating others or answering or asking questions. Personal-identity motives manifest as an expression of sentiment (for example, anger or outrage). Entertainment motives are characterised by a wish to inject humour into, or elicit enjoyment from, a discussion. Social-interaction-based motives for writing comments centre on relationship building, as they manifest in comments that sympathise, leave condolences or applaud good work by the content producer (for example, the journalist on a news website) or other commentators (Diakopoulos and Naaman 2011; Springer et al. 2015; Barnes 2014).

Other scholars have found that performance factors into the motivation to leave comments (Livingstone 2008; Dholakia et al. 2004; Papacharissi 2002). In this case the writing of a comment enables identity to be built, managed and interpreted, in what Goffman (1959) refers to as a "performance of self".

Of significance to the studies outlined is that while they are useful in outlining the types of comments we may make, they still only focus on one facet that impacts on the actual behaviour, rather than the many and varied factors. They also fail to take into account, that we will not always behave in the same way—there are multiple individual factors and factors associated with the environment in which we are commenting that will influence our behaviour.

THE OUTLAWS

Another method of investigating online commenting is by examining broad classifications of behaviour. Significantly, much attention has been paid to those who are not commenting, but are instead "lurking". Lurking refers to the behaviour of viewing messages or member contributions but not posting anything. "Lurkers" are found to make up the majority of members of online communities (Preece et al. 2004; van Djik 2009; Ling et al. 2005). Lurkers have been viewed as the free-riders of a community, but Wasko and Faraj (2005) argue they contribute purely through the act of viewing comments. Hampton (2016) further argues that these individuals may be passive in their information collection, but the persistent and ambient nature of digital conversations means these individuals may act on this information at a later date.

Viewing, as a vital component of online discussion, individuals who are not leaving a visible marker of their interaction with a comment is more in line with Crawford's (2009) argument that an understanding of the existence of a cadre of "background listeners" is necessary to provoke online disclosures. Without an awareness that there is someone listening, even if those listeners may not be flagging their presence by leaving a comment or even Liking a status update, we have no motivation to leave comments. Indeed, my own research of users of alternative journalism websites found that a significant portion of individuals visiting the sites were "engaged listeners" (Barnes 2016). When reading the comments but not necessarily leaving a comment of their own, engaged listeners develop an affective relationship with both the website and other commenters, similar to the relationships between fans, the objects of their fandom and fan communities. Those who are reading our comments are vital members of the online communities in which we are making comments and we cannot begin to understand the complex mechanicians contributing to our behaviour in these spaces unless we consider how they contribute to these communities.

Of course, not all online behaviour is a positive interaction. Anti-social online behaviour can range from impoliteness and incivility, to behaviours such as flaming and trolling, to more extreme behaviours such as online harassment. Impoliteness refers to behaviours not adhering to etiquette or established normative behaviours and includes name-calling, aspersion, pejorative speech and vulgarity (Papacharissi 2004). Impoliteness is closely linked to incivility. Incivility is differentiated as a "set of behaviors that threaten democracy, deny people their personal freedoms and stereotype social groups" (Papacharissi 2004, p. 267). Hutchens et al. (2015) further defines incivility in relation to discussion as making blatant attacks on a person's beliefs and character, as opposed to being critical of that person's opinions. However, what each individual classifies as incivility can differ (Reader 2012), making it a difficult concept to define and police.

Academic research has further described hostile, aggressive and abusive messages that threaten another internet user as "flaming" (see Hutchens et al. 2015): "The process of 'flaming' thus includes the creation, transmission, and interpretation of a message that is perceived from multiple perspectives as violating norms" (O'Sullivan and Flanagin 2003, p. 85). This negatively perceived behaviour is also widely described as "trolling". However, Herring et al. (2002, p. 372) differentiate trolling from flaming by describing trolling as the luring of others into useless, circular discussion, while Hardaker (2010, p. 237) describes a troll as someone

> who constructs the identity of sincerely wishing to be part of the group in question, including professing, or conveying pseudo-sincere intentions, but whose real intention(s) is/are to cause disruption and/or to trigger or exacerbate conflict for the purposes of their own amusement.

Whitney Phillip's (2015) examination of trolling behaviour is useful to point out here. As she notes, any type of online aggression or antagonistic commentary can be ubiquitously referred to as trolling, however it is a very explicit type of online behaviour. Indeed, Phillip's definition of trolling is particularly useful as it is based on those who self-identify as trolls and partake in highly stylised practices. For Phillips, a troll is someone who deliberately disrupts online interactions and derives amusement from another's anger. This behaviour though, cannot be viewed in isolation, as "trolls are engaged in a grotesque pantomime of dominant cultural tropes" (Phillips 2015, p. 8). Trolls are a reflection of social and cultural trends and while their behaviour is roundly criticised, they employ similar techniques to social media marketers and dominant media institutions. Trolling as a behaviour, then, is the product of multiple factors. Likewise, so are all forms of commenting behaviour and we must situate any examination of this behaviour within wider subjectivities.

The most extreme form of anti-social behaviour is defined as online harassment or the "intentional infliction of substantial emotional distress accomplished by online speech that is persistent enough to amount to a course of conduct rather than an isolated incident" (Citron 2014, p. 3). Targets of harassment are subjected to threats of violence, privacy invasions, lies intended to cause reputational harm, calls for strangers to physically harm them and technological attacks. However, despite the significant social, cultural and economic impacts of online harassment, it is generally dismissed as an internet problem, something that we expect and dismiss.

All anti-social behaviours are generally associated with the anonymity facilitated by online interactions. Anonymity, because it can curb social inhibitions, has been associated with incivility and hostility online (Reader 2012; Hardaker 2010; Alonzo and Aiken 2004). As attention is turned to mitigating offensive behaviour, many newspaper websites, in particular, have moved to limit or remove the ability to anonymously comment (see Reader 2012). However, anonymity has also been shown to have significant benefits for online participation. Meyer and Carey (2014) found that it was the ability of participants to comment anonymously combined with the presence of an active moderator that encouraged frequent participation, rather than a pervading sense of civility in the comment threads. Anonymity has also been shown to increase participation in forums focused on health issues (Tanis 2008) and political activism (Stieglitz 2006; Tanner 2001) and helps people in online support groups to disclose intimate problems and concerns that they may not feel comfortable discussing with their friends and family (Scott et al. 2011). How, then, are we to balance the goal of broad participation with that of maintaining a safe, non-hostile environment for online discussion?

TRACING ONLINE RELATIONSHIPS

One way to investigate the culture of commenting is to examine how we structure our relationships and therefore our online networks. This approach focuses on relationships between people, rather than on the individuals' personal attributes (Borgatti et al. 2014). The individuals who we interact with on social media or other participatory websites can be understood as being connected to us through weak, strong or latent ties.

Much of our online activity is undertaken with people to whom we have weak ties (Granovetter 1973; boyd and Ellison 2007). When we connect with people to whom we have weak ties, we may know them casually or not at all offline, but their presence can enhance our online experience by increasing our knowledge and/or providing a sense of camaraderie (Heatherly et al. 2016; Barker et al. 2015). We communicate with people to whom we have weak ties through platforms that provide for more limited forms of communication (mainly group-wide media, such as social networking sites). This is because interactions between weakly tied people are more passive—for example, simply Liking a Facebook post (Haythornthwaite 2005). However, the technical affordances of online spaces such as Facebook enable a persistence in articulation and contact, meaning we can maintain social ties with individuals with whom we may have lost contact prior to these technologies (for example, school friends or colleagues from previous jobs) (Hampton 2016).

Weak ties differ from so-called strong ties, which are restricted to groups of people who share a physical space and are linked by other ties that include kinship (Parks 2011, p. 107). We use a variety of communication methods to interact with our strong ties, including group-wide media, such as social networking sites, and person-to-person communications, such as private meetings and personal emails. This is because we have a greater need to communicate with our strong ties using a variety of expressions, so we will proactively seek out other means of communication (Haythornthwaite 2005).

Finally, latent ties are those with people who are unknown to us, but with whom there is a potential to forge a relationship (Borst et al. 2017) or those with whom, as Haythornthwaite (2005, p. 137) notes, relationships are "technically possible but not yet activated". These ties can be formed when we are reading and writing comments on participatory websites such as news websites, e-commerce sites or content communities. We may also form latent ties with friends of friends on social networking sites, as messages and Likes can appear on the timelines of as-yet-unconnected users.

THE ONLINE COMMUNITY

Examining commenting through the lens of relationships and the variations in our network structures leads to understanding our online interactions in the context of community, or the study of social structure. Ultimately if we are to mitigate against antagonistic and aggressive comments then we need to understand this behaviour as a social problem, not an internet problem. Placing comments as interactions that take place within a community helps do this.

As Hampton (2016, pp. 103–104) notes,

> intrinsic to the study of community is the exploration of the variation in relational strength, social contexts, and the cleavages that exist between ties and the environments where they are formed and maintained.

To examine online interactions in this way, we turn to the concept of the "virtual community", which has transformed the notion of "communities" from densely knit neighbourhood groups into groups that may be geographically dispersed personal networks.

Many scholars have used the traditional geographic community as a framework for defining the characteristics of online communities. In these studies, the focus is on shared interests, facilities, values and experiences; mutual obligations; and social interaction (Chen and Hung 2010; Hopkins et al. 2004; Tyler 2006; Nip 2004). As a result, much work has investigated how online relationships impact on the nature and character of offline community relationships (Shen and Cage 2015; Rosenberry 2010; Putnam 2001; Blanchard and Horan 2000). As Rheingold (1993, p. 62) notes, online communities develop in "response to the hunger for community that has followed the disintegration of traditional communities". This approach, however, privileges the offline community by failing to attribute benefits to online communities in their own right. As Norris (2002, pp. 11–12) notes, "online participation has the capacity to deepen linkages among those sharing similar beliefs as well as serving as a virtual community that cuts across at least some traditional social divisions". An easy way to reconfigure the concept of community is consider that online groups meet in shared spaces. Those meeting online consider the platforms on which they meet to be shared spaces which facilitate not only interactions but shared resources and support, shared identities and interpersonal relationships (Baym 2015). Over time, then, theorists have moved away from conceptualising community in terms of physical connectivity or geography to conceptualising it as based on the psychological engagement and quality of sociality: "In this 'weak' sense, community is viewed as culture, a set of ideas and interpersonal sentiments" (Parks 2011, p. 107).

Drawing on Anderson's (1991) notion of the "imagined community" is a useful method for articulating online communities. For Anderson, essential in the formation of nation-states was that a community must be able to "imagine" its members as a mental construct through the sharing of commonalities. Without being able to meet each member of their national community physically, individuals relied on the mass media, which created connections between language, place and ideology, to build their imagination of other members of the community. In Anderson's account, newspapers, in particular, informed the collective understanding that there was a "steady, anonymous, simultaneous experience" of a newspaper-reading community (Anderson 1991, p. 31). Communities that are formed online are articulated in similar ways—through ideas, values and culture shared via platforms where members can not only directly interact with others, but also imagine a wider reading community (Litt 2012). Viewed in this way, rather than asking whether online communities are authentic, scholars influenced by Andersen have argued for looking at "the style in which they are imagined" (Anderson 1991, p. 6). For Baym (1998) an online community's style is shaped by external contexts, infrastructure systems, group purposes and participant characteristics. Therefore, if we are to understand commenting as taking place in a community, then the community's style, which is made up of all these factors will influence our commenting behaviour. Understood in this way, comments are not made in a vaccum. We are not inherently predisposed to a particular behaviour, be that a troll, lurker or fanboy, but rather will alter our behaviour based on which community we are commenting in.

Yet there is still resistance to claims that all of our group interactions online can be classified as constituting an online community. Bury's (2016) investigation of fan activities on social networking sites, such as Facebook, Twitter and Tumblr, found that they did not constitute the formation of online fan communities as newsgroups and Listserv once did. This, she argues, is due to the technological limitations of these platforms, which discourage in-depth interactivity. In contrast, Parks (2011) found that a group that gathers in one of these spaces "might qualify" as an online community if its members engaged in collective action, shared in rituals, had a variety of relational linkages and were emotionally bonded to at least some other members in a way that conferred a sense of belonging and group identification. These characteristics correlate with the broader literature on community development and are concepts an individual uses to help define his or her community when clear spatial boundaries do not exist, creating a "sense of virtual community" (Blanchard et al. 2011).

Using this concept of an online community, it is possible to view discussions online as having the ability to create a sense of virtual community. Individuals would, however, be required to create, personalise and visit profiles regularly, make social contacts and respond to other users in some way (Parks 2011). Understood in this way, though, an individual who does not leave a visible marker of his or her presence, such as an engaged listener (Barnes 2016), would not be considered a part of the community. Given the networked nature of our online relationships, which include not only strong and weak ties, but also latent ties, this limitation would fail to account for a fundamental part of the social structures enabled by these technologies. Drawing such a stark line between our online and offline worlds is also problematic when you consider that each impacts upon the other. What we do in the "real world" has implications for our behaviour online and likewise what we do online will influence our offline behaviour.

Hampton's (2016) assertion that the technological affordances of digital media, and social media in particular, have fundamentally changed our conception of community and the enduring nature of social ties is useful, then, in addressing this concern. He argues that we have entered a period of metamodernity, in which we have a persistent-pervasive community construct. Through the affordances of digital communication technologies, persistent contact is enabled because our relationships, and the social contexts where they are formed, are less transitory and therefore less likely to dissolve with geographical and life-stage differences. Pervasive awareness is also enabled, allowing for an easy, informal watchfulness that provides for sustained closeness and information exchange. Given that "[s]cholars have always linked the study of community to understanding the social implication of new technology" (Hampton 2016, p. 104), the concept of the online community is essential in understanding the participatory culture of commenting. An online community, then, encompasses shared forms of interactions, social ties among members and a sense of belonging and group identification—a sense of community. It is this final component that enables the capture of more "passive" members in the persistent-pervasive online community.

McMillan and Chavis (1986) outlined four dimensions needed to develop a sense of community: membership, influence, fulfilment of needs and shared emotional connection. Membership relates to feeling part of the community, which is determined by "in" and "out" groups. Influence encompasses both an individual's ability to influence the community and the community's ability to exert influence on its members. Fulfilment of needs creates a sense of togetherness, making interaction rewarding. Shared emotional connection is created through shared history, frequent contact, quality interaction and personal investment. Drawing on these sense-of-community characteristics, Gibbs et al. (2016) found very little variation in sense of community across more or less active participants. Thus, lurkers and engaged listeners can form part of an online community if they develop a sense of belonging. Understanding comments as taking place within online communities is therefore vital if we are to understand not only the factors that influence our behaviour, but all the contributors that influence that community.

Trading in Social Capital

As a method of understanding how individuals facilitate and sustain community development, community scholars draw on Bourdieu's (1986) concept of social capital, which refers to the ways in which an individual draws value from his or her social relationships in the communal environment.

Putnam (2001) takes this concept further, outlining that social capital is divided into "bridging social capital" or "bonding social capital". Bridging social capital is created when we are exposed to networks where the majority of our connections are weak ties. That is, social capital that is based on connection rather than close friendship (Ellison et al. 2011). Given that bridging social capital binds a diverse group, it provides opportunities for access to diverse opinions and information, but offers little emotional or substantive support. In contrast, bonding social capital is typically related to close connections such as family and friends, or strong ties, and offers little diversity in information or opinions. As these close connections are based on repeated and frequent interactions, they excel at providing emotional and substantive support.

This structural perspective of social capital is further explicated in Burt's (2005) model of brokerage and closure. Brokerage occurs when people build connections between otherwise unconnected individuals, increasing access to heterogeneous, rather than redundant, information and resources. Brokerage, then, is the structural mechanism that produces bridging social capital. Closure occurs when an individual connects to others who are already connected among themselves. Because an individual's views, information and resources are more likely to resonate with close friends and family than those of strangers, closure tends to reinforce existing opinions and behaviours, while also providing trust and support. Closure demonstrates how bonding social capital can be demonstrated in social structures.

Many scholars have found that one's social capital increases as a result of online activity (Castells 2013; Ellison et al. 2011; Lee and Lee 2010; Davenport and Daellenbach 2011). Online, bridging social capital, particularly through social networking sites, has been shown to increase due to the affordances enabling diverse network maintenance and information flows (Ellison et al. 2007). However, other scholars have shown that, due to the intimate nature of sharing on these platforms, relationship ties are strengthened, resulting in higher levels of bonding social capital (Marwick and boyd 2011). When individuals who operate in online spaces begin to see those spaces as communities, they have been found to experience greater levels of trust (Blanchard et al. 2011) and support (Blanchard and Lynne Markus 2004), and increased loyalty to the site itself (Barnes 2014; Lin 2008)—indicating bonding social capital. An increase in bonding social capital at the expense of bridging social capital can create tensions, however. While a strengthening of relational ties—increased bonding social capital—could enhance an individual's support network, it could also result in closed and less-inclusive online communities, as they will not be open to more diversity (Shen and Cage 2015).

Understanding the online platforms in which we conduct our commenting behaviour as facilitating community is an important way to not only understand why we behave the way we do, but also our individual responsibilities in creating inclusive online spaces. We all have a vital role to play in creating safer and kinder spaces for online interactions. Group interactions within an established community can help establish norms that dictate how individuals are expected to behave within those groups (Kiesler et al. 2011; Honeycutt 2005; Blanchard 2004). Specifically, participants can collectively challenge and castigate the writers of hostile or abusive comments. Kaigo and Watanabe (2007, p. 1262) found an online forum to be self-regulating where posts of questionable morality were routinely denounced and marginalised by other commentators, such that "the user community functioned pro-socially in an uncontrolled, anonymous Internet forum". The use of these "scapegoats" helps establish group norms by creating a membership boundary, clearly indicating who is "in" and who is "out" (McMillan and Chavis 1986). In this way, an online community enacts a form of "concertive control" that, through consensus, helps regulate behaviour, enhance a sense of online community and increase participation (Gibbs et al. 2016). Normative influence, or a tendency to conform to the positive expectations of others (Burnkrant and Cousineau 1975), also influences an individual's behaviour. For example, providing support publicly for other members of a community encourages others to reciprocate and also provide support by sharing information, giving advice and offering reassurance (Blanchard et al. 2011). Other scholars have found that normative influences and concertive control have a pro-social impact, working to bind members together and ensure the community endures (Gibbs et al. 2016; Aakhus and Rumsey 2010).

> Cohesive communities cohere not just around supportive communication, but also due to a powerful system of peer-based concertive control and normative influence in which members internalise group norms and act in accordance with them. (Gibbs et al. 2016, p. 18)

Significantly, even hard forms of discipline have been found to enhance bonding, rather than alienate members, because they create a heightened sense of accountability and investment (Gibbs et al. 2016).

A ROLE FOR THE LANDSCAPE

While the community or peer-based concertive control (and therefore each individual) has a role to play in establishing an online community's norms, which then impact upon the behaviours exhibited in those communities, normative behaviour can also be dictated by technological affordances and institutional policies. Game communities offer some of the best examples of this. Recognised as notoriously toxic cultures, game publishers have been successful in modifying governance through technological affordances and policies to influence the shared values and norms of their communities. These shifts have had a significant impact in managing anti-social behaviour (this argument is elaborated on in Chap. 5).

Couldry's (2010) conception of "voice" and "landscape" offers much in the way of understanding how individuals, technology and the institutions who control the platforms on which we interact inform the online participatory environment. The concept of "voice" comprises "not just in the 'individuals' speaking, but also the 'landscape' in which they speak and are, or are not, heard" (Couldry 2010, p. 114). Under this paradigm, the platform, be it a participatory website or social media, is a central constituent of this landscape, and the individuals are those who choose to comment within it. Additionally, within the context of online commenting, the landscape is not only the website itself, but the factors that regulate participation, such as the moderation policies associated with user-produced content, the interfaces used by readers to upload their comments and curation measures that determine what content readers see. These landscape factors, or what this book will refer to as "institutional factors", because they are controlled by the institutions who own the commenting platforms, have been shown to have a significant impact on the participatory behaviours of the audience (Meyer and Carey 2014; de Souza and Preece 2004; Reich 2011) and can influence participants' willingness to interact (Kiesler et al. 2011; Honeycutt 2005; Blanchard 2004).

Moderation of comments can either happen prepublication, by screening comments before they appear, or postpublication, by retroactively removing comments that are reported. Wise et al. (2006) suggest that moderation makes readers more comfortable with the idea of participating in online forums. Moderation, however, may have a negative impact by eliciting a resistance to the predominant viewpoint expressed in comment threads. Sherrick and Hoewe (2016) examined explicit comment moderation on news websites and found that readers often associated this with censorship of a particular viewpoint (that which differed from the editorial stance and the views of other commenters). When faced with this perceived censorship, individuals were defensive, suggesting moderation may elicit a negative emotional response within the comment thread. Moderation and policies on anonymity are often employed to address uncivil behaviour on message boards, with numerous studies showing that moderation is associated with higher levels of civility (Coe et al. 2014; Diakopoulos and Naaman 2011; Ruiz et al. 2011). Likewise, limiting anonymity has been found to create more civil online interactions, because in groups where posters are not allowed to participate anonymously, participants understand group norms better and are more likely to adhere (Blanchard et al. 2011). However, anonymity may increase participation (Meyer and Carey 2014). In another example of institutional policy influencing participatory behaviour, Wikipedia introduced a three-day revert rule (which meant an editor could only revert an article back to his or her own preferred version three times a day) to end so-called "edit-wars" (Kittur et al. 2007).

Equally, the specifics of the interface accessed by people leaving comments can impact upon the frequency and type of participation within an online community. Within these spaces, usability, which is defined by what happens at the human-computer interface, is a key factor in enhancing or inhibiting sociability through discussion (de Souza and Preece 2004). Specifically, the design of the interface can affect how community members communicate, how they react to one another, the kind of behaviour that occurs, and the satisfaction that individuals derive from belonging to a particular online community (de Souza and Preece 2004).

Kiesler et al. (2011) makes a series of recommendations for site design to influence normative behaviours and mitigate anti-social behaviours. These include altering how information is displayed by moving inappropriate posts, determined as such through a user-scoring system, to places they are less likely to be seen or degrading comments through techniques of disemvowelling.

Highlighting preferred behaviour through reputation profiles and rewards, and applying throttles or activity quotas to limit repetitive behaviour were also recommended. User registration was also found to mitigate uncivil behaviour. These recommendations are based on the premise that "less tangible, softer, and more behavioral remedies may be desirable to try first" (2011, p. 167). If these interventions fail, harsher interventions such as public rebukes, gags or bans can be used.

The curation of content, either by an individual or an algorithm, will also impact upon commenting behaviour. Curation differs from moderation in that it is not specifically removing comments, but highlighting particular comments or directing specific content at specific individuals—a form of network-to-person communication. Curation that privileges particular information or limits exposure to unique or non-conforming information may reduce opinion quality and diversity. Hampton (2016) has suggested that algorithms could even enhance network closure by limiting exposure to diversity and removing the advantage afforded by a network structured around weak and latent ties—thus fundamentally changing the social structures of our online communities. Curation, then, will impact upon our commenting behaviour as it can impact upon our access to content and relationships that inform the feedback loop of our interactions.

Overall, then, if we are to fully comprehend why we behave the way we do online then we must situate our online interactions within a community. If we do this then we can take into account the individual and peer-based factors that will enhance and alter our behaviour. The community framework also points to the institutions that control the platforms on which we comment as having a fundamental role to play in helping to create harmonious and inclusive communities. They can exert influence over anti-social behaviours through the use of moderation policies, interface design and curation.

Conclusion: Understanding Commenting Behaviour Is Contingent upon Placing Them in a Community

In charting the online commenting landscape, this chapter has argued that how we behave online is influenced by a complex system of factors, and it is only by understanding all of these factors and how they interconnect that we can truly understand commenting culture. Understanding our online interactions as taking part in online communities provides a framework for understanding the social implications of commenting. The use of the online community frames interactions as being based on relationships and social structures. Based on this premise, we then have a method for understanding how we as individuals and collectively can influence the behaviour of others online. Importantly, understanding our online interactions as taking place within a community forces us to expect the same social norms and values that we do of interactions offline. This is vital if we are to ensure more pro-social interactions and mitigate against some of the more troubling anti-social behaviour. There is nothing virtual about online interaction. It is as real as the off-line community in its benefits and consequences.

Institutional factors such as moderation, the user interface and the algorithms employed by the platforms that host the communities in which we choose to comment influence our behaviour. This suggests that the responsibility for creating an inclusive and civil community online rests with both individuals and the institutions that manage these platforms. In returning to the Wild West analogy invoked in the introduction, there are roles for individual heroes and institutional lawmen in tackling antagonistic and aggressive behaviour.

The following chapters will continue to elaborate on this concept by outlining the specific factors that influence online commenting behaviour and how they relate to both individual and institutional responsibilities to create harmonious and civil online communities. Next, we will draw on fan studies to investigate the role of emotion and affect as triggers for participation, and how they impact upon group interactions online. This approach will also shed light on how we adapt and change our behaviour according to our level of affective investment.

REFERENCES

Aakhus, Mark, and Esther Rumsey. 2010. Crafting Supportive Communication Online: A Communication Design Analysis of Conflict in an Online Support Group. *Journal of Applied Communication Research* 38 (1): 65–84.

Alonzo, Mei, and Milam Aiken. 2004. Flaming in Electronic Communication. *Decision Support Systems* 36 (3): 205–213.

Anderson, Benedict. 1991. *Imagined Communities. Reflections on the Origin and Spread of Nationalism*. London/New York: Verso.

Barker, Valerie, David M. Dozier, Amy Schmitz Weiss, and Diane L. Borden. 2015. Harnessing Peer Potency: Predicting Positive Outcomes from Social Capital Affinity and Online Engagement with Participatory Websites. *New Media & Society* 17 (10): 1603–1623. https://doi.org/10.1177/1461444814530291.

Barnes, Renee. 2014. The 'Ecology of Participation': A Study of Audience Engagement on Alternative Journalism Websites. *Digital Journalism* 2 (4): 542–557.

———. 2016. The Ecology of Participation. In *The SAGE Handbook of Digital Journalism*, ed. Tamara Witschge, Chris Anderson, David Domingo, and Alfred Hermida, 179–191. New York: Sage.

Baym, Nancy K. 1998. The Emergence of On-Line Community. In *Cybersociety 2.0: Revisiting Computer-Mediated Community and Technology*, ed. Steve Jones, 35–68. Thousand Oaks/London/New Delhi: Sage.

———. 2015. *Personal Connections in the Digital Age*. Cambridge/Malden: Polity.

Beer, David. 2008. Social Network(ing) Sites … Revisiting the Story So Far: A Response to Danah boyd & Nicole Ellison. *Journal of Computer-Mediated Communication* 13 (2): 516–529.

Blanchard, Anita. 2004. Virtual Behavior Settings: An Application of Behavior Setting Theories to Virtual Communities. *Journal of Computer-Mediated Communication* 9 (2). http://jcmc.indiana.edu/vol9/issue2/blanchard.html.

Blanchard, A.L., and T. Horan. 2000. Virtual Communities and Social Capital. In *Social Dimensions of Information Technology: Issues for the New Millennium*, ed. G.D. Garson, 5–20. Hershey: Idea Publishing Group.

Blanchard, Anita L., and M. Lynne Markus. 2004. The Experienced Sense of a Virtual Community: Characteristics and Processes. *ACM Sigmis Database* 35 (1): 64–79.

Blanchard, Anita L., Jennifer L. Welbourne, and Marla D. Boughton. 2011. A Model of Online Trust: The Mediating Role of Norms and Sense of Virtual Community. *Information, Communication & Society* 14 (1): 76–106.

Borgatti, Stephen P., Daniel J. Brass, and Daniel S. Halgin. 2014. Social Network Research: Confusions, Criticisms, and Controversies. In *Contemporary Perspectives on Organizational Social Networks*, 1–29. Bingley: Emerald Group Publishing Limited.

Borst, Irma, Christine Moser, and Julie Ferguson. 2017. From Friendfunding to Crowdfunding: Relevance of Relationships, Social Media, and Platform Activities to Crowdfunding Performance. *New Media & Society*. https://doi.org/10.1177/1461444817694599.

Bourdieu, Pierre. 1986. The Forms of Capital. In *Handbook of Theory and Research for the Sociology of Education*, ed. John G. Richardson, 241–258. New York: Greenwood Publishing Group.

boyd, Danah M., and N.B. Ellison. 2007. Social Network Sites: Definition, History, and Scholarship. *Journal of Computer-Mediated Communication* 13 (1): 210–230.

Burnkrant, Robert E., and Alain Cousineau. 1975. Informational and Normative Social Influence in Buyer Behavior. *Journal of Consumer Research* 2 (3): 206–215.

Burt, Ronald S. 2005. *Brokerage and Closure: An Introduction to Social Capital.* Oxford: Oxford University Press.

Bury, Rhiannon. 2016. Technology, Fandom and Community in the Second Media Age. *Convergence. The International Journal of Research into New Media Technologies*: 1–16. https://doi.org/10.1177/1354856516648084.

Carpini, Michael X. Delli, Fay Lomax Cook, and Lawrence R. Jacobs. 2004. Public Deliberation, Discursive Participation, and Citizen Engagement: A Review of The Empirical Literature. *Annual Review of Political Science* 7: 315–344.

Castells, Manuel. 2013. *Communication Power.* Oxford: Oxford University Press.

Chen, Chih-Jou, and Shiu-Wan Hung. 2010. To Give or To Receive? Factors Influencing Members' Knowledge Sharing and Community Promotion in Professional Virtual Communities. *Information & Management* 47 (4): 226–236.

Citron, Danielle Keats. 2014. *Hate Crimes in Cyberspace.* Cambridge, MA: Harvard University Press.

Coe, Kevin, Kate Kenski, and Stephen A. Rains. 2014. Online and Uncivil? Patterns and Determinants of Incivility in Newspaper Website Comments. *Journal of Communication* 64 (4): 658–679.

Conover, Michael D., Bruno Gonçalves, Alessandro Flammini, and Filippo Menczer. 2012. Partisan Asymmetries in Online Political Activity. *EPJ Data Science* 1 (1): 1.

Couldry, Nick. 2010. *Why Voice Matters: Culture and Politics After Neoliberalism.* London/California/New Delhi/Singapore: Sage.

Crawford, Kate. 2009. Following You: Disciplines of Listening in Social Media. *Continuum: Journal of Media & Cultural Studies* 23 (4): 525–535.

Davenport, Sally, and Urs Daellenbach. 2011. Belonging to a Virtual Research Centre: Exploring the Influence of Social Capital Formation Processes on Member Identification in a Virtual Organization. *British Journal of Management* 22 (1): 54–76.

De Souza, Clarisse Sieckenius, and Jenny Preece. 2004. A Framework for Analyzing and Understanding Online Communities. *Interacting with Computers* 16 (3): 579–610.

Dholakia, Utpal M., Richard P. Bagozzi, and Lisa Klein Pearo. 2004. A Social Influence Model of Consumer Participation in Network-and-Small-Group-Based Virtual Communities. *International Journal of Research in Marketing* 21 (3): 241–263.

Diakopoulos, Nicholas, and Mor Naaman. 2011. *Towards Quality Discourse in Online News Comments.* Proceedings of the ACM 2011 Conference on Computer Supported Cooperative Work. Hangzhou, China.

Dvir-Gvirsman, Shira. 2016. Media Audience Homophily: Partisan Websites, Audience Identity and Polarization Processes. *New Media & Society.* https://doi.org/10.1177/1461444815625945.

Ellison, N., C. Steinfield, and C. Lampe. 2007. The Benefits of Facebook "Friends": Exploring the Relationship Between College Students' Use of Online Social Networks and Social Capital. *Journal of Computer-Mediated Communication* 12 (3): 1143–1168.

Ellison, Nicole B., Charles Steinfield, and Cliff Lampe. 2011. Connection Strategies: Social Capital Implications of Facebook-Enabled Communication Practices. *New Media & Society* 13 (6): 873–892.

Gibbs, Jennifer L., Heewon Kim, and Seol Ki. 2016. Investigating the Role of Control and Support Mechanisms in Members' Sense of Virtual Community. *Communication Research*: 1–29. https://doi.org/10.1177/0093650216644023.

Goffman, Erving. 1959. *The Presentation of Self in Everyday Life*. Garden City: Doubleday.

Granovetter, Mark S. 1973. The Strength of Weak Ties. *American Journal of Sociology* 78(6): 1360–1380.

Habermas, Jurgen. 1984. *The Theory of Communicative Action*. Trans. Thomas McCarthy. *Reason and the Rationalization of Society*. Vol. 1. Boston: Beacon press.

Hampton, Keith N. 2016. Persistent and Pervasive Community: New Communication Technologies and the Future of Community. *American Behavioral Scientist* 60 (1): 101–124.

Hardaker, Claire. 2010. Trolling in Asynchronous Computer-Mediated Communication: From User Discussions to Academic Definitions. *Journal of Politeness Research* 6 (2): 215–242.

Haythornthwaite, Caroline. 2005. Social Networks and Internet Connectivity Effects. *Information, Community & Society* 8 (2): 125–147.

Heatherly, Kyle A., Lu Yanqin, and Jae Kook Lee. 2016. Filtering Out the Other Side? Cross-Cutting and Like-Minded Discussions on Social Networking Sites. *New Media & Society*. https://doi.org/10.1177/1461444816634677.

Herring, Susan, Kirk Job-Sluder, Rebecca Scheckler, and Sasha Barab. 2002. Searching for Safety Online: Managing "Trolling" in a Feminist Forum. *The Information Society* 18 (5): 371–384.

Holbert, R. Lance, R. Kelly Garrett, and Laurel S. Gleason. 2010. A New Era of Minimal Effects? A Response to Bennett and Iyengar. *Journal of Communication* 60 (1): 15–34.

Honeycutt, Courtenay. 2005. Hazing as a Process of Boundary Maintenance in an Online Community. *Journal of Computer-Mediated Communication* 10 (2): np.

Hopkins, Liza, Julian Thomas, Denise Meredyth, and Scott Ewing. 2004. Social Capital and Community Building Through an Electronic Network. *Australian Journal of Social Issues* 39 (4): 369.

Hutchens, Myiah J., Vincent J. Cicchirillo, and Jay D. Hmielowski. 2015. How Could You Think That?!?!: Understanding Intentions to Engage in Political Flaming. *New Media & Society* 17 (8): 1201–1219.

Hwang, Hyunseo, Youngju Kim, and Yeojin Kim. 2016. Influence of Discussion Incivility on Deliberation an Examination of the Mediating Role of Moral Indignation. *Communication Research.* https://doi.org/10.1177/0093650 215616861.

Kaigo, Muneo, and Isao Watanabe. 2007. Ethos in Chaos? Reaction to Video Files Depicting Socially Harmful Images in the Channel 2 Japanese Internet Forum. *Journal of Computer-Mediated Communication* 12 (4): 1248–1268.

Kaplan, Andreas M., and Michael Haenlein. 2010. Users of the World, Unite! The Challenges and Opportunities of Social Media. *Business Horizons* 53 (1): 59–68.

Kiesler, Sara, Robert Kraut, Paul Resnick, and Aniket Kittur. 2011. Regulating Behavior in Online Communities. In *Building Successful Online Communities: Evidence-Based Social Design*, ed. Robert Kraut and Paul Resnick, 125–178. Cambridge, MA: MIT Press.

Kittur, A., B. Suh, B.A. Pendleton, and E.H. Chi. 2007. *He Says, She Says: Conflict and Coordination in Wikipedia*. CHI 07: Proceedings of the ACM Conference on Human Factors in Computing Systems, 453–462. New York: ACM Press.

Knobloch-Westerwick, Silvia, and Benjamin K. Johnson. 2014. Selective Exposure for Better or Worse: Its Mediating Role for Online News' Impact on Political Participation. *Journal of Computer-Mediated Communication* 19 (2): 184–196.

Knobloch-Westerwick, Silvia, and Jingbo Meng. 2011. Reinforcement of the Political Self Through Selective Exposure to Political Messages. *Journal of Communication* 61 (2): 349–368.

Lee, Hyunjoo, and Junghee Lee. 2010. Computer-Mediated Communication Network: Exploring the Linkage Between Online Community and Social Capital. *New Media & Society* 12: 711–728.

Lin, Hsiu-Fen. 2008. Determinants of Successful Virtual Communities: Contributions from System Characteristics and Social Factors. *Information & Management* 45 (8): 522–527.

Ling, Kimberly, Gerard Beenen, Pamela Ludford, Xiaoqing Wang, Klarissa Chang, Xin Li, Dan Cosley, Dan Frankowski, Loren Terveen, and Al Mamunur Rashid. 2005. Using Social Psychology to Motivate Contributions to Online Communities. *Journal of Computer-Mediated Communication* 10 (4): Article 10. https://doi.org/10.1111/j.1083-6101.2005.tb00273.x.

Litt, Eden. 2012. Knock, Knock. Who's There? The Imagined Audience. *Journal of Broadcasting & Electronic Media* 56 (3): 330–345.

Livingstone, Sonia. 2008. Taking Risky Opportunities in Youthful Content Creation: Teenagers' Use of Social Networking Sites for Intimacy, Privacy and Self-Expression. *New Media & Society* 10 (3): 393–411.

Lowrey, Wilson. 2006. Mapping the Journalism-Blogging Relationship. *Journalism* 7 (4): 477–500.

Marwick, Alice E., and Danah boyd. 2011. I Tweet Honestly, I Tweet Passionately: Twitter Users, Context Collapse, and the Imagined Audience. *New Media & Society* 13 (1): 114–133.

McMillan, David W., and David M. Chavis. 1986. Sense of Community: A Definition and Theory. *Journal of Community Psychology* 14 (1): 6–23.

Messing, Solomon, and Sean J. Westwood. 2012. Selective Exposure in the Age of Social Media: Endorsements Trump Partisan Source Affiliation When Selecting News Online. *Communication Research.* https://doi. org/10.1177/0093650212466406.

Meyer, Hans K., and Michael Clay Carey. 2014. In Moderation: Examining How Journalists' Attitudes Toward Online Comments Affect the Creation of Community. *Journalism Practice* 8 (2): 213–228.

Mutz, Diana C. 2006. *Hearing the Other Side: Deliberative Versus Participatory Democracy.* New York: Cambridge University Press.

Nip, Joyce Y.M. 2004. The Relationship Between Online and Offline Communities: The Case of the Queer Sisters. *Media, Culture & Society* 26 (3): 409–428.

Norris, P. 2002. *The Virtuous Citizen.* Oxford: Oxford University Press.

O'Sullivan, Patrick B., and Andrew J. Flanagin. 2003. Reconceptualizing 'Flaming' and Other Problematic Messages. *New Media & Society* 5 (1): 69–94.

Papacharissi, Zizi. 2002. The Presentation of Self in Virtual Life: Characteristics of Personal Home Pages. *Journalism & Mass Communication Quarterly* 79 (3): 643–660.

———. 2004. Democracy Online: Civility, Politeness, and the Democratic Potential of Online Political Discussion Groups. *New Media & Society* 6 (2): 259–283.

Parks, Malcolm R. 2011. Social Network Sites as Virtual Communities. In *A Networked Self: Identity, Community, and Culture on Social Network Sites*, ed. Zizi Papacharissi, 105–123. London: Routledge.

Phillips, Whitney. 2015. *This Is Why We Can't Have Nice Things: Mapping the Relationship Between Online Trolling and Mainstream Culture.* Cambridge, MA: The MIT Press. eBook Collection (EBSCOhost), EBSCOhost. Accessed 12 Sept 2017.

Preece, Jenny, Blair Nonnecke, and Dorine Andrews. 2004. The Top Five Reasons for Lurking: Improving Community Experiences for Everyone. *Computers in Human Behavior* 20 (2): 201–223.

Putnam, Robert D. 2001. *Bowling Alone: The Collapse and Revival of American Community.* New York: Simon and Schuster.

Rainie, L., and A. Smith. 2012. Social Networking Sites and Politics (Dataset). *Pew Internet.* http://pewinternet.org/Reports/2012/Social-networking-and-politics.aspx. Accessed 13 Sept 2016.

Reader, Bill. 2012. Free Press vs. Free Speech? The Rhetoric of "Civility" in Regard to Anonymous Online Comments. *Journalism & Mass Communication Quarterly* 89 (3): 495–513.

Reich, Zvi. 2011. User Comments: The Transformation of Participatory Space. In *Participatory Journalism: Guarding Open Gates at Online Newspapers*, ed. Jane B. Singer, David Domingo, Ari Heinonen, Alfred Hermida, Steve Paulussen, Thorsten Quandt, Zvi Reich, and Marina Vujnovic, 96–117. West Sussex: Wiley.

Rheingold, Howard. 1993. *The Virtual Community: Finding Connection in a Computerized World*. London: Addison-Wesley Longman Publishing Co., Inc.

———. 2000. *The Virtual Community: Homesteading on the Electronic Frontier*. Boston: MIT Press.

Rosenberry, Jack. 2010. Virtual Community Support for Offline Communities Through Online Newspaper Message Forums. *Journalism & Mass Communication Quarterly* 87 (1): 154–169.

Ruiz, Carlos, David Domingo, Josep Lluís Micó, Javier Díaz-Noci, Koldo Meso, and Pere Masip. 2011. Public Sphere 2.0? The Democratic Qualities of Citizen Debates in Online Newspapers. *The International Journal of Press/Politics* 16 (4): 463–487.

Scheufle, Dietram A., and Patricia Moy. 2000. Twenty-Five Years of the Spiral of Silence: A Conceptual Review and Empirical Outlook. *International Journal of Public Opinion Research* 12 (1): 3–28.

Scott, C.R., S.A. Rains, and M. Haseki. 2011. Anonymous Communication: Unmasking Findings Across Fields. In *Communication Yearbook*, ed. C. Salmon, 299–342. New York: Routledge.

Shen, Cuihua, and Charles Cage. 2015. Exodus to the Real World? Assessing the Impact of Offline Meetups on Community Participation and Social Capital. *New Media & Society* 17 (3): 394–414.

Sherrick, Brett, and Jennifer Hoewe. 2016. The Effect of Explicit Online Comment Moderation on Three Spiral of Silence Outcomes. *New Media & Society*. https://doi.org/10.1177/1461444816662477.

Springer, Nina, Ines Engelmann, and Christian Pfaffinger. 2015. User Comments: Motives and Inhibitors to Write and Read. *Information, Communication & Society* 18 (7): 798–815.

Stieglitz, Eric J. 2006. Anonymity on the Internet: How Does It Work, Who Needs It, and What Are Its Policy Implications. *Cardozo Arts & Entertainment Law Journal* 24: 1395.

Stroud, Natalie Jomini. 2010. Polarization and Partisan Selective Exposure. *Journal of Communication* 60 (3): 556–576.

Tanis, Martin. 2008. Health Related On-Line Forums: What's the Big Attraction? *Journal of Health Communication* 13 (7): 698–714.

Tanner, Eliza. 2001. Chilean Conversations: Internet Forum Participants Debate Augusto Pinochet's Detention. *Journal of Communication* 51 (2): 383–403.

Tyler, Richard. 2006. Comprehending Community. *Critical Studies* 28 (1): 21–28.

van Dijck, José. 2009. Users Like You? Theorizing Agency in User-Generated Content. *Media, Culture & Society* 31 (1): 41–58.

Wasko, Molly McLure, and Samer Faraj. 2005. Why Should I Share? Examining Social Capital and Knowledge Contribution in Electronic Networks of Practice. *MIS Quarterly* 29 (1): 35–57.

Wise, Kevin, Brian Hamman, and Kjerstin Thorson. 2006. Moderation, Response Rate, and Message Interactivity: Features of Online Communities and Their Effects on Intent to Participate. *Journal of Computer-Mediated Communication* 12 (1): 24–41.

Wojcieszak, Magdalena E., and Diana C. Mutz. 2009. Online Groups and Political Discourse: Do Online Discussion Spaces Facilitate Exposure to Political Disagreement? *Journal of Communication* 59 (1): 40–56.

CHAPTER 2

You Either Love It or You Hate It! The Emotional and Affective Factors of Commenting

[F]andom is everywhere and all the time, a central part of the everyday lives of consumers operating within a networked society.
Jenkins (2007, p. 361)

Fan studies is at the forefront of exploring the audience's engagement and participation with a media text. When Henry Jenkins released his highly influential book *Textual Poachers: Television Fans and Participatory Culture* in 1992, it heralded the establishment of fan studies as a field of research. Jenkins rejected what he called the media-fostered stereotype that fans are "cultural dupes, social misfits and mindless consumers" (p. 23) and instead argued that fans are active producers and manipulators of meanings. He insisted that fans cease to simply be an audience for a popular text and become active participants who appropriate and interpret a text before recirculating it within the fan community. In this way, Jenkins defined fans as:

Readers who appropriate popular texts and reread them in a fashion that serves their different interests, as spectators who transform the experience of watching television into a rich and complex participatory culture. (1992, p. 23)

Now, more than 20 years later, with the arrival of new technologies and platforms (as outlined in the previous chapter), scholars still draw on this work to study online communities of fans, as fandom offers "rich insights into media consumption, identity, textual engagement and communications" (Bennett 2014a, p. 6).

There is a substantial body of work that has investigated specific fan communities on online forums (see for example Baym 2000; Bury 2005; Gatson and Zweerink 2004) and social media (see for example Bennett 2014b; Bury 2016; Deller 2011; Kalviknes Bore and Hickman 2013; Highfield et al. 2013; Jenkins et al. 2013; Marwick et al. 2014; Wood and Baughman 2012). Indeed, as the quotation at the beginning of this chapter suggests, Jenkins has continued to richly explore how aspects of participatory culture, in particular transmedia storytelling and the blurring of the lines between producers and consumers, impacts on fan culture. In *Convergence Culture*, Jenkins (2006) suggests a mainstreaming of fannish behaviour and situates fans as early adopters of the behaviours associated with convergence. Historically, fans were seen as exemplary resistant readers of mainstream media, as typifying a subversion of cultural power. As Fiske (2002) pronounced, fans create a "semiotic democracy" that makes sense of texts in creative, personal and communal ways that challenge existing power hierarchies.

New media technologies that facilitate creating one's own content, and platforms such as social media that enable that content to be easily shared, provide avenues for these fannish behaviours to easily infiltrate our everyday communications and relationships, suggesting that fandom provides a framework for understanding each individual's role in challenging traditional communication structures. Fandom, when considered as a collective action rather than an individual behaviour, is characterised by (1) a focus on the community that forms around that object of fandom and (2) the social interactions that occur there (Busse and Gray 2011). Given that these are also two structural models facilitated by social media, an understanding of fandom is useful for a broader understanding of participatory behaviour. Yet individual fannish behaviours that focus on affective investment and engagement with a text also provide insight into our actions in a participatory environment.

To investigate the participatory culture of commenting, fan studies offers much towards understanding the playful, committed and emotional engagements that can be generated through interaction in a online community. While fan studies is typically concerned with a particular object of fandom—a television show, for example—and the community that forms around that object, an examination of fannish behaviours and how and why fans engage in these communities can move us towards understanding online behaviour more generally. As Gray et al. (2007, p. 10) argue, investigation of the intrapersonal pleasures and motivations of fans enables scholars to unpack and better understand the social, cultural and economic transformations of our time:

> Studying fan audiences allows us to explore some of the key mechanisms through which we interact with the mediated world at the heart of our social, political, and cultural realities and identities.

Being a fan, then, has become a common mode of cultural, social and political consumption and, this being the case, the study of fandom cannot be relegated to subcultures that focus on a particular object of fandom, but should be viewed as a way to understand how we enact our identity and how communities can form.

This chapter will draw on the rich and extensive theoretical underpinnings of fan studies to explore factors that inform our online commenting behaviour. Drawing on the fundamental and interconnected areas of fandom—including creative production, belonging and identity, play and pleasure, and emotion and affect—it will chart some of the influences that drive us to make comments, and the investment that even "lurkers", or those simply reading the comments, make in online communities.

CO-OPTING, CREATIVE PRODUCTION AND SPREADABILITY

Central to Jenkins' (1992) understanding of fans is the idea that they are active producers and manipulators of meanings. Fans cease to be simply an audience for a popular text and become active participants who appropriate and interpret a text before recirculating it within the fan community. Within this process, however, it is not just the creation of content inspired by the object of fandom, but also the sharing of knowledge and the information exchange that are central to fan culture. In this way fans become "textual poachers" by co-opting the object of their fandom, creatively producing their own interpretations and then sharing them with others in the fan community.

Lancaster (2001) uses a similar method to consider fans, but instead of focusing on their "poaching", he sees the fan as a textual performer. His study focuses on the TV series *Babylon 5* and the activities of online fans, fan-fiction writers and those who engage in role-playing games. Lancaster emphasises the significance of fan emotion and considers fan culture to be articulated through creative self-expression, as well as communal activities. Therefore, for Lancaster, to be a fan, one must perform by creating content through fan fiction or involving oneself in communal discussions about the object of fandom.

These broad ways of understanding fans can equally be applied to the act of commenting online. Comments are not made in a vacuum. They are made in response to particular content—for example, a journalist's article on a news website, a status update, a video, a meme or another piece of creative content that is shared on social media. As commenters, we are appropriating that original "text" and creating our own meanings and interpretations. Therefore, a comment, to draw on Lancaster's work, could be viewed as a performance of self, used as a method of not only self-expression, but also identity construction.

There is a danger in this fan-studies approach of focusing on creative production at the expense of other, less-visible forms of engagement. Given that those listening or "lurking" make up a significant portion of our online communities, we must also examine their role in engagement. Green and Jenkins (2011) have approached this task by focusing on spreadable media—the content that we choose to share and circulate within our networks.

We as individuals ascribe value and worth to content through its circulation. New meanings are imbued through the act of spreading, as, when we read, listen or view material that has been shared by someone in our network, we think about not only how to interpret the producer's meaning, but also what the person who forwarded it to us is trying to communicate.

> Choosing to spread media involves a series of socially embedded decisions: that the content is worth watching; that it is worth sharing with others; that the content might interest specific people we know; that the best way to spread that content is through a specific channel of communication; and, often, that the content should be circulated with a particular message attached. (Green and Jenkins 2011, pp. 113–114)

However, even if there is no message offering an interpretation attached, the sharing of material implies to the reader that the sharer has interpreted and prescribed meaning to that material in some way. The mere act of clicking on, for example, a Like button or a technological affordance that enables sharing to our network could become a mechanism of participatory culture. Using this framework, those who are lurking in our online communities are still undertaking an active process of meaning making ensuring they are part of the participatory process at play in online communities.

When understood in this way, the writing of a comment is a form of performance that is used for identity construction—another key factor in fandom that will be covered next. The simple act of sharing content, even without adding an interpretation or comment, ascribes value and invites interpretation. Readers of this content are not only interpreting the shared content, but also the intent and intended meaning of the sharer. This active interpretation of meaning becomes a method of binding and building a community.

BELONGING AND IDENTITY

As outlined in the previous chapter, a sense of belonging is vital to creating and sustaining an online community. This sense of belonging, or sense of community, is created through the development of a collective identity for the community, and fan studies offers much towards understanding how identity and belonging influence the reading and writing of comments.

Fiske (1992) has argued that fans are driven by a desire not only to produce meaning and pleasure from popular culture, but also to connect with and define a fan community, and themselves within that community. For Fiske (1992, p. 30) the pleasure of "meaning-making" underlines the experience of the fan:

> All popular audiences engage in varying degrees of semiotic productivity, producing meanings and pleasures that pertain to their social situation out of the products of the cultural industries. But fans often turn this semiotic productivity into some form of textual production that can circulate among—and thus help define—the fan community.

Fandom exemplifies the idea that we will choose different interpretative communities based on our individual processes of meaning making (Busse and Gray 2011). An interpretation of an object of fandom will often be contested, and specific communities develop around a repertoire of interpretative strategies. It may be a reading consensus—for example, a consensus for a pairing of characters that may not be romantically involved in the original text—or just an agreement on a definition of good writing. In the same way, we will choose news websites not just based on the content but also on the perceived audience of that site (Dvir Gvirsman 2016). We actively seek out communities of people we believe to be "like-minded". Our meaning-making is then a process of determining our group interactions.

Meaning-making and its role in forming collective identity is not just for those who actively contribute. Fans who are not explicitly interacting with a fan community, but are undertaking their fannish activities in isolation, can be participating in an imagined community of other fans, creating parasocial relations with other fans (Busse and Gray 2011). Indeed, readers or lurkers of the comment threads that follow news stories have been shown to develop a sense of community with other commenters (Barnes 2014). I have previously described these community members as "engaged listeners" (Barnes 2014).

"Listening" is the broad mode of practice that can be used to understand how the "silent majority" consume much of the information that is circulated online. It incorporates the practice of "background listening" (Crawford 2009) where "commentary and conversations continue as a backdrop throughout the day, with only a few moments requiring concentrated attention" (Crawford 2009, p. 528). However, listening can also incorporate a more complex process whereby the content (for example a news story and content provided by other commenters) is used to garner a sense of belonging to the online community and facilitate identity development (Barnes 2014). People who might be termed "engaged listeners" may have emotional or personal reactions to the content, but they will not publicly declare this; instead, they will remain silent and internalise their response. However, they are negotiating their own identity and forming a sense of connection to the collective audience through visiting the site.

Collective identity development within a fan community is not always positive, however. Many fan scholars (Hills 2002; Dell 1998; Harris 1998; Jancovich 2002) have highlighted how fan communities reflect existing social and cultural hierarchies, as the choice of fan object and the practices of fan consumption constitute a reflection of the distribution of social, cultural and economic capital (Bourdieu 1986). These scholars found that interpretive communities of fandom are embedded in existing structures of the status quo. Therefore, when fans come together, they do not just form a community, but they also form a social hierarchy where they can compete over knowledge, access to the object of fandom and status. This has implications for how we understand the communities that form on online forums, social media and even news websites. Commenting and interacting on these sites may be methods of connecting with a community of other readers and commenters and establishing oneself within that community's hierarchy. This will then influence the establishment of normative behaviours within a particular community (Gibbs et al. 2016), with the hierarchy exerting concertive control and establishing what is acceptable commenting behaviour. Where one fits, then, within that social hierarchy will dictate the type of commenting behaviour undertaken.

While this collective identity can help form a sense of belonging, there is also a role for individual identity play. For example, Sandvoss (2005) argues that the act of being a fan is narcissistic, since it relies on a perception (either consciously or unconsciously) that parts of the self are in the external object—the source of the fandom:

> As the fabric of our lives is constituted through constant and staged performances, the self becomes a performed, and hence symbolic, object. In this sense fandom is not an articulation of inner needs or drives, but is itself constitutive of the self. Being a fan in this sense reflects and constructs the self. (2005, p. 48)

Using the example of sports fans, Sandvoss outlines how any text can be used to project and affirm our own values and sense of self. For example, sports fans will fashion their teams in their images, viewing teams as nationalistic if they see themselves as nationalists, or as diverse and multicultural if they see themselves that way. This formation of self through engagement with an object in the public space, whether that be popular culture, news or other online interactions, is significant. Sandvoss, therefore, offers a useful approach to identifying the nature of commenting online. This approach enables an alternative view of participation, as it helps to locate the role of expression in the project of self-formation. A comment is a form of expression and therefore could be viewed as an attempt to define and construct a particular presentation of self. However, when it is in response to another comment or stimulus content, we will attribute to that content a predetermined meaning that affirms our sense of self—which may differ from another's process of meaning making and interpretation of that content. Social networking sites have been shown to be particularly effective platforms for presenting the self because they provide the means to do so—profiles—and the ability, through networks of

contacts, to extend that presentation to a performance, in which comments and interactions are public displays to our connections. As
Papacharissi (2010, p. 105) notes:

> Individual and collective identities are presented and promoted. Online
> social networks … reinforce the social affordances of online environments,
> by fostering interaction that is primarily interpersonal, and founded upon
> the norms of everyday interaction.

Online environments, then, allow us to signal our social identities to
others through the selection of objects—groups to join, websites to
view—as well as the content that we share. As Liu (2007, p. 252) notes,
"cultural consumption not only 'echoes' but also actively 'reinforces' who
one can be".

The interplay of belonging and identity is therefore an important factor
when considering commenting culture. It plays a role in forming behavioural expectations in the community and informs our own projects of the
presentation of self through performance. Two more central factors in the
study of fans are the elements of pleasure and play.

PLEASURE AND PLAY

Understanding the roles of both pleasure and play in how we read and
write comments online offers much towards a broader understanding of
why we behave the way we do. Booth (2010) argues, in his investigation
of digital fandom, that fan activities are informed by a "philosophy of playfulness". This "philosophy of playfulness" helps enable the enactment of
the mediated communities of fans. Specifically, he uses the example of
ludic comments on blogs to illustrate how humorous and playful interaction forms a basis of fan culture online. However, the role of pleasure and
play in fans enacting of communities can be applied to online behaviours
more broadly. As Booth (2010, p. 2) notes:

> More so than at any other time, the media we use in our everyday lives has
> been personalized, individualized, and made pleasurable to use.

Following Habermas' (1991) outline of the "ideal" public sphere,
which emphasised separation of the private and the public to ensure freedom for the individual to develop the self without state interference, many

scholars have lamented the personalisation or trivialisation of the media (McKee 2005 provides a comprehensive overview of this argument). As a result, many scholars question the value of online participatory culture, particularly online comments, in political discourse because of the propensity for the inclusion of the personal and trivial (Reich 2011; Shepard 2011; Singer and Ashman 2009; Bird 2011). Within this Habermasian-framed analysis, critical, rational discourse is attributed to political discussion, while fan-based discussion, as a site of intense pleasure and play, contributes emotional or "irrational" discourse.

This distinction, however, is problematic and not reflective of how we engage online. Drawing on a study of people leaving comments on news and political blogs, Gray (2007) posits that this focus on news or political discussion as serving a primarily informational purpose (and not being a pleasurable experience) is the result of studies focused on news production, rather than on people who use news, and is an "idealised discussion of what the news should do" (2007, p. 77) rather than of what it does. Therefore, the play- and pleasure-seeking behaviours traditionally associated with fandom need to be considered when examining all commenting, regardless of the content being commented on.

In an attempt to measure the role of pleasure in undertaking online activities, many scholars (for an overview see Barker et al. 2015) have drawn on flow theory, which defines the mental state of pleasure that an individual will reach when immersed in a specific activity (Csikszentmihalyi 1975). Flow encompasses playfulness as a response to a pleasurable activity that involves intense engagement. Flow occurs when there is a balance in the level of skill required to undertake an activity and the challenge afforded by that activity. A flow state can be achieved in media consumption when there is a balance between the individual's cognitive abilities (the skill to interpret meanings associated with the particular media) and the challenge provided by the messages contained within that media (Sherry 2004). The reading of comments may be understood in the same way—as the consumption of other media—and, therefore, flow would be related to this activity. Writing comments and engaging in discussion online can equally be understood as generating and sustaining a flow state. Indeed, Barker et al. (2015) found that, when an individual participates in an online community, makes recommendations or discusses information with other online users, online enjoyment and engagement are heightened and the experience of flow is facilitated. Flow and the associated playfulness can help explain the immersion that occurs when we are engaged in online discussion. A humorous and extended interaction with members of a social media network may be the result of achieving a flow state. Likewise, ongoing trolling in a comment thread could also be attributed to this immersive state. As Herring et al. (2002) and Hardaker (2010) note, trolls seek to lure others into useless, circular discussion for their own amusement, suggesting a flow state.

We can see, then, that the fan-like behaviours of pleasure and play, just like those of creative production and identity construction, inform online commenting culture. All of these fannish behaviours, however, are informed by the affective investment fans devote to the object of their fandom (Grossberg 1992; Hills 2002).

AFFECTIVE INVESTMENT

Affect has been studied by scholars from various disciplines including neurology, sociology, psychology, and media and cultural studies. Broadly, the affective dimension of something refers to the spectrum of subjective reactions we are less conscious of than our emotions. It is possible to name an emotion and pin it down, but the affective tone of an experience is harder to label (Veale 2013).

There are two dominant theoretical interpretations of affect (Seigworth and Gregg 2010, p. 5). The first is based on understanding affect as a social and sometimes collective director of energy or engagement (Deleuze 1988 in Seigworth and Gregg 2010). The second is more concerned with affect as an emotional and psychological gratification and centres on a catalogue of specific affects (Tomkins 1995).

For Grossberg (1992), drawing on the work of Deleuze (1988), fandom can be understood as a particular form of emotional intensity or "affect". He uses the term "affect" to describe the meaning inspired by feeling. The affect that a media text inspires in a fan helps him or her negotiate the level of investment in that text. It is possible, then, to be a "casual fan" and only invest a small level of passion and energy into some texts, but also a more dedicated fan who invests a higher level of emotional attachment in a different text. Overall, though, emotion is a cornerstone for inspiring engagement with a text.

Psychologist Silvan Tomkins, however, argues that there is a basic set of affects, including shame, interest, surprise, joy, anger, fear, distress and disgust, that operate as a motivational system (Sedgwick and Frank 1995,

p. 5). Understood in this way, emotion is the feeling, while affect is the physical response to the feeling.

Scholarly work on affect, therefore, tends to build on one of these specific notions of affect. However, Wetherell's (2012) work in this field attempts to draw from both theoretical positions to produce a more flexible affective framework, rather than one determined by lines of causation, character types or neat emotion categories. Wetherell (2012, p. 4) argues that "affect" is embodied meaning-making that is commonly understood as human emotion.

Fandom can be understood as a particular form of "affect" (Grossberg 1992; Hills 2002) inspired by a media text, which is then mobilised in negotiating the level of investment in that text. Typically, affect is used as a method of analysing engagement with visual texts such as television. For example, Hills (2005) has examined horror fandom's consumption of certain types of texts for the purpose of arousing the particular affect of fear. Likewise, Gorton (2009), in her work on the emotional response of the television audience, draws on affect theory to fundamentally challenge the notion that knowledge is gained solely through rational objectivity, and argues for the place of emotion in decision-making.

However, many argue that emotion and affect play a role in engagement beyond popular culture. Scholars in the field of fan activism and political participation have already pointed to the role affective properties associated with popular culture can have in political discourse (Marcus et al. 2000; van Zoonen 2005; Jenkins and Shresthova 2012). Liesbet van Zoonen (2005) examines how fan cultures display numerous traits of ideal citizenship. She argues against the binary that suggests audiences of fans are brought into being by entertainment, while politics, and therefore political communication, produces publics composed of citizens. Emotion and affective intelligence, she argues, are essential in engaging the public's reason and judgement in all communication.

Therefore, we can understand our commenting behaviour online as informed by our affective investment in both discussion and the online community in which it takes place. As Gibbs (2011, p. 263) notes, the "internet appropriates some of the features of intimate conversations", enabling a use of the personal to influence wider social, cultural and political discourses on a local, national and even global scale.

Wetherell's (2012) concept of "affective practice", whereby an emotional reaction to a particular stimuli produces an emotion and subsequent action, offers much to understanding our commenting behaviours. Within this model, communication involves an attempt to produce emotion, where a general feeling is aroused from engagement with the text and, as a result, we may have a physical reaction to that emotion. Understood in this way, engagement with and production of a text such as a comment can be investigated as grounded in affect (Gorton 2009; Probyn 2005; Riley 2005; Gibbs 2011). The concept of "affective practice" offers two approaches to the exploration of commenting culture. Firstly, there may be an emotional reaction or a feeling of being caught up in the "affective practice" that is encouraged by the website content or other commenters. Secondly, a particular "affective practice" can also inspire action, such as the leaving of a comment.

Gibbs' (2011) notion of "affect contagion" provides a method for understanding the momentum or spread of particular affects. "Affect contagion", Gibbs (2011) argues, is responsible for the traction of particular "events" that are mediated by the media. In particular, some affects, particularly anger, fear and enjoyment, are highly contagious and can form a feedback loop.

Applying "affect contagion" to the act of writing a comment, it could be argued that each affective contribution by a commenter can inspire further affective contributions from others in a feedback loop. It is possible, then, to explore the darker, anti-social comments and how contributors can feed each other. Input from a particularly angry or hostile commenter will inspire further angry and hostile comments from others in a feedback loop. On news websites, Hutchens et al. (2015) found that commenters were more likely to flame other commenters if they viewed aggression as acceptable. If angry and hostile comments are established as the norm, this will suggest that aggression is acceptable. This form of aggression has been defined as reactive aggression, which is aggression that is initiated in response to a perceived threat (Hutchens et al. 2015; Crick and Dodge 1996; Dodge and Coie 1987). Reactive aggression differs from proactive aggression, which is goal-directed and a deliberative form of aggression motivated by external rewards (Dodge 1991). Reactive aggression is the result of hostile attribution bias (Dodge and Coie 1987) which occurs when we interpret a person's comments (or intentions) as hostile, even if the person had no intention of being hostile (Crick and Dodge 1996). People then leave hostile comments if they perceive a threat against themselves or a group they identify with (for example, due to political preference, or religious or social affiliation) (Hutchens et al. 2015).

Therefore hostility (even if only perceived) will inform an affective contagion ensuring an ongoing feedback loop of hostile comments.

Affect, a central factor in the study of fans, therefore can be understood as a driver of commenting. It can inform the investment needed to take the action of commenting, but can also inform how we understand the ongoing nature of hostile and aggressive comments. Anti-fan or non-fan studies offer further understanding of the more anti-social behaviours in comment threads.

THE ANTI-FAN AND THE NON-FAN

Gray (2003, p. 70) has argued that the anti-fan, or an individual who "strongly dislikes(s) a given text or genre, considering it inane, stupid, morally bankrupt and/or aesthetic drivel", demonstrates an equivalent affective investment to the fan. Using the example of the TV sitcom *The Simpsons*, Gray (2003) outlines that anti-fans are distant readers of the text, never watching the programme, but developing affective relationships with it through paratexts.

Paratexts are anything that surrounds a text and helps an individual evaluate it. Media talk, conversations, spoilers or even advertisements would constitute a paratext, and, from these, the anti-fan constructs meanings and attributes values and expectations to the text.

> Behind dislike, after all, there are always expectations—of what a text should be like, of what is a waste of media time and space, of what morality or aesthetics texts should adopt. (Gray 2003, p. 73)

Much like fan activity, anti-fan activity is described as being organised (Gray 2003, p. 71), and involving creative production (Gray 2005, p. 847) and a type of performance (2005, p. 845). Therefore, studies of anti-fandom can offer much towards understanding anti-social commenting behaviour.

Negative comments following a social media status-update, news story or blog post may be understood as less about the content of the original post and more about the contextuality of that individual, which has been established by the paratexts that he or she has used to create an understanding of a particular topic. For example, news organisations have often equated uncivil comments following a news story with contributors who have not read the story (Lichterman 2017). Other studies have shown that only news that is deemed relevant and involves the reader will encourage comments (Diakopoulos and Naaman 2011), and domestic political news receives the most comments (Weber 2014).

By understanding these comments within the frameworks of anti-fandom, then, it is possible to pinpoint the paratexts that inform this behaviour. It should be noted that drawing on anti-fan frameworks is not an attempt to excuse what Jane (2014, p. 186) has referred to as "hateful discourse, which involves excessively threatening, violent, or sexually violent rhetoric; attempts to incite violence or criminal action in the real world; and/or the causing of harm to 'ordinary' people or vulnerable groups", but rather to sketch contributing factors to the participatory culture of commenting.

Gray (2003) has also pointed to the importance of "non-fans"—those who view or read a text rarely, but still find it meaningful. Non-fans, he argues, are the comfortable majority, and can even include fans who may be lax fans—those who may watch a television programme when they can, rather than keeping up with every episode. Non-fandom, then, involves "considerable flow in and out of different viewing positions" (Gray 2003, p. 74) and can offer further frameworks for understanding online commenting behaviours. When we are online, we are also offline, and therefore how we engage with a text, or what Gray terms our "viewing position", will be impacted by the physical, social and cultural factors at play in that offline world (this concept will be explored further in the following chapter).

CONCLUSION: FINDING THE FAN IN COMMENTS

This chapter has explored how fan studies can inform our understanding of commenting culture. Scholars have moved to understand fans as coming in many different shapes and sizes. Abercrombie and Longhurst (1998, p. 14) outlined a spectrum of people with a positive involvement with a text or object of fandom from "fan" to "petty producer". Sandvoss (2005, p. 7) has argued that fans should be identified not by the objects of their fandom, but by their fan practices:

> The clearest indicator of a particular emotional investment in a given popular text lies in its regular repeated consumption, regardless of who its reader is and regardless of the possible implications of this affection.

Sandvoss contends that the subcultures that evolve around a given media text or genre are based on regular and emotionally committed consumption. As such, fan theory applies to members of these subcultural groups, even if the groups do not describe themselves as fans. The key point here is that it is not the object of fandom that defines the fan, but the level of investment in that object and the activities associated with that investment. As Sandvoss (2005, p. 3) suggests, fandom is a common and ordinary aspect of everyday life, and, therefore, any fan consumption "becomes a generally understood language through which one's identity is communicated and assessed". It is therefore possible to use a fan-studies framework to understand online commenting culture more broadly, rather than in relation to a specific object of fandom.

Specifically, fan studies provide some important clues to the factors that influence online commenting culture. Commenters are involved in a form of creative production that is informed by a philosophy of playfulness. Online discussions can generate and sustain a "flow state" (Csikszentmihalyi 1975) in which pleasure is the cornerstone of their immersion in the practice. Commenters contributing to an online discussion do so as part of a process of defining not only the collective identity of the community in which they are commenting, but also the performance of the self. This complex process of identity construction is not the sole province of active contributors, but also applies to the lurkers, or those merely reading the comments. Those who form the "listening" public of comments can still use this engagement as a form of identity development and form an affective relationship with the community in which the comments are made.

Overall, the emphasis in fan studies on the affective investment of fans offers much towards understanding why we make comments and even the investment those reading the comments make in online communities. Commenting can be understood as an "affective practice" whereby we are driven to comment by the emotion elicited from stimulus content. This affective practice can either be positive or negative and may be informed by an affective contagion, where affective contributions are inspired by others in a feedback loop.

Taken as a whole, this fan-based approach enables a more comprehensive grasp of audience engagement in which emotion and affect are among the triggers for participation. Through the use of anti-fan and non-fan classifications, fan studies has also provided an understanding that we may move between different "viewing positions" and levels of affective investment.

In the next chapter, we will continue to explore how we may adapt and change our online behaviours based on "viewing positions" or situational factors.

REFERENCES

Abercrombie, Nicholas, and Brian J. Longhurst. 1998. *Audiences: A Sociological Theory of Performance and Imagination*. London: Sage.

Barker, Valerie, David M. Dozier, Amy Schmitz Weiss, and Diane L. Borden. 2015. Harnessing Peer Potency: Predicting Positive Outcomes from Social Capital Affinity and Online Engagement with Participatory Websites. *New Media & Society* 17 (10): 1603–1623.

Barnes, Renee. 2014. The 'Ecology of Participation': A Study of Audience Engagement on Alternative Journalism Websites. *Digital Journalism* 2 (4): 542–557.

Baym, Nancy K. 2000. *Tune In, Log On: Soaps, Fandom, and Online Community*. Vol. 3. Thousand Oaks: Sage.

Bennett, Lucy. 2014a. Tracing Textual Poachers: Reflections on the Development of Fan Studies and Digital Fandom. *The Journal of Fandom Studies* 2 (1): 5–20.

———. 2014b. 'If We Stick Together We Can Do Anything': Lady Gaga Fandom, Philanthropy and Activism Through Social Media. *Celebrity Studies* 5 (1–2): 138–152.

Bird, Susan E. 2011. Seeking the Audience for News Response, News Talk, and Everyday Practices. In *The Handbook of Media Audiences*, ed. Virginia Nightingale, 489–508. Malden: Wiley.

Booth, Paul. 2010. *Digital Fandom: New Media Studies*. Vol. 68. New York: Peter Lang.

Bourdieu, Pierre. 1986. The Forms of Capital. In *Handbook of Theory and Research for the Sociology of Education*, ed. John G. Richardson, 241–258. New York: Greenwood Publishing Group.

Bury, Rhiannon. 2005. *Cyberspaces of Their Own: Female Fandoms Online*. Vol. 25. New York: Peter Lang.

———. 2016. Technology, Fandom and Community in the Second Media Age. *Convergence: The International Journal of Research into New Media Technologies*: 1–16. https://doi.org/10.1177/1354856516648084.

Busse, Kristina, and Jonathan Gray. 2011. Fan Cultures and Fan Communities. In *The Handbook of Media Audiences*, ed. Virginia Nightingale, 425–443. Malden: Wiley.

Crawford, Kate. 2009. Following You: Disciplines of Listening in Social Media. *Continuum: Journal of Media & Cultural Studies* 23 (4): 525–535.

Crick, Nicki R., and Kenneth A. Dodge. 1996. Social Information-Processing Mechanisms in Reactive and Proactive Aggression. *Child Development* 67 (3): 993–1002.

Csikszentmihalyi, Mihaly. 1975. *Beyond Boredom and Anxiety*. San Francisco: Jossey-Bass.

Deleuze, G. 1988. *Spinoza: Practical Philosophy*. Trans. Robert Hurley. San Francisco: City Light Books.

Dell, C.E. 1998. Lookit That Hunk of a Man: Subversive Pleasures, Female Fandom and Professional Wrestling. In *Theorizing Fandom. Fans, Subculture, and Identity*, ed. Cheryl Harris and Alison Alexander. Cresskill: Hampton Press.

Deller, Ruth. 2011. Twittering on: Audience Research and Participation Using Twitter. *Participations* 8 (1): 216–245.

Diakopoulos, Nicholas, and Mor Naaman. 2011. *Towards Quality Discourse in Online News Comments*. Proceedings of the ACM 2011 Conference on Computer Supported Cooperative Work. Hangzhou, China.

Dodge, Kenneth A. 1991. *The Structure and Function of Reactive and Proactive Aggression*. In Earlscourt Symposium on Childhood Aggression, June, 1988. Toronto: Lawrence Erlbaum Associates, Inc.

Dodge, Kenneth A., and John D. Coie. 1987. Social-Information-Processing Factors in Reactive and Proactive Aggression in Children's Peer Groups. *Journal of Personality and Social Psychology* 53 (6): 1146–1158.

Dvir Gvirsman, Shira. 2016. Media Audience Homophily: Partisan Websites, Audience Identity and Polarization Processes. *New Media & Society*. https://doi.org/10.1177/1461444815625945.

Fiske, John. 1992. The Cultural Economy of Fandom. In *The Adoring Audience: Fan Culture and Popular Media*, ed. Lisa A. Lewis, 30–49. London: Routledge.

———. 2002. *Television Culture*. London/New York: Routledge. Original edition, 1987.

Gatson, Sarah N., and Amanda Zweerink. 2004. *Interpersonal Culture on the Internet: Television, the Internet, and the Making of a Community*. Wales: Edwin Mellen Press.

Gibbs, A. 2011. Affect Theory and Audience. In *The Handbook of Media Audiences*, ed. Virginia Nightingale, 251–266. Malden: Wiley.

Gibbs, Jennifer L., Heewon Kim, and Seol Ki. 2016. Investigating the Role of Control and Support Mechanisms in Members' Sense of Virtual Community. *Communication Research*. https://doi.org/10.1177/0093650216644023.

Gorton, Kristyn. 2009. *Media Audiences: Television, Meaning and Emotion*. Edinburgh: Edinburgh University Press.

Gray, Jonathan. 2003. New Audiences, New Textualities Anti-fans and Non-fans. *International Journal of Cultural Studies* 6 (1): 64–81.

———. 2005. Antifandom and the Moral Text: Television Without Pity and Textual Dislike. *American Behavioral Scientist* 48 (7): 840–858.

Gray, Jonathan Alan. 2007. The News You Gotta Love It. In *Fandom: Identities and Communities in a Mediated World*, ed. Jonathan Alan Gray, Cornel Sandvoss, and C. Lee Harrington, 75–87. New York: NYU Press.

Gray, Jonathan Alan, Cornel Sandvoss, and C. Lee Harrington. 2007. *Fandom: Identities and Communities in a Mediated World*. New York: NYU Press.

Green, Joshua, and Henry Jenkins. 2011. Spreadable Media: How Audiences Create Value and Meaning in a Networked Economy. In *The Handbook of Media Audiences*, ed. Virginia Nightingale. Malden: Wiley.

Grossberg, L. 1992. The Affective Sensibility of Fandom. In *The Adoring Audience: Fan Culture and Popular Media*, ed. Lisa A. Lewis, 60–65. London: Routledge.

Habermas, Jürgen. 1991. *The Structural Transformation of the Public Sphere: An Inquiry into a Category of Bourgeois Society*. Cambridge: MIT Press.

Hardaker, Claire. 2010. Trolling in Asynchronous Computer-Mediated Communication: From User Discussions to Academic Definitions. *Journal of Politeness Research* 6 (2): 215–242.

Harris, Cheryl. 1998. A Sociology of Television Fandom. In *Theorizing Fandom: Fans, Subculture, and Identity*, ed. Cheryl Harris and Alison Alexander. Cresskill: Hampton Press.

Herring, Susan, Kirk Job-Sluder, Rebecca Scheckler, and Sasha Barab. 2002. Searching for Safety Online: Managing "Trolling" in a Feminist Forum. *The Information Society* 18 (5): 371–384.

Highfield, Tim, Stephen Harrington, and Axel Bruns. 2013. Twitter as a Technology for Audiencing and Fandom: The #Eurovision Phenomenon. *Information, Communication & Society* 16 (3): 315–339.

Hills, Matt. 2002. *Fan Cultures*. London: Routledge.

———. 2005. *The Pleasures of Horror*. London: Bloomsbury Publishing.

Hutchens, Myiah J., Vincent J. Cicchirillo, and Jay D. Hmielowski. 2015. How Could You Think That?!?!: Understanding Intentions to Engage in Political Flaming. *New Media & Society* 17 (8): 1201–1219.

Jancovich, Mark. 2002. Cult Fictions: Cult Movies, Subcultural Capital and the Production of Cultural Distinctions. *Cultural Studies* 16 (2): 306–322.

Jane, Emma A. 2014. Beyond Antifandom: Cheerleading, Textual Hate and New Media Ethics. *International Journal of Cultural Studies* 17 (2): 175–190.

Jenkins, Henry. 1992. *Textual Poachers: Television Fans and Participatory Culture*. New York: Routledge.

———. 2006. *Convergence Culture: Where Old and New Media Collide*. New York: New York University Press.

———. 2007. Afterword: The Future of Fandom. In *Fandom: Identities and Communities in a Mediated World*, ed. Jonathan Alan Gray, Cornel Sandvoss, and C. Lee Harrington, 357–364. New York: NYU Press.

Jenkins, Henry, and Sangita Shresthova. 2012. Up, up, and away! The power and potential of fan activism. *Transformative Works and Cultures*, 10 (Special issue): np. http://dx.doi.org/10.3983/twc.2012.0435.

Jenkins, Henry, Sam Ford, and Joshua Green. 2013. *Spreadable Media: Creating Value and Meaning in a Networked Culture*. New York: NYU Press.

Kalviknes Bore, Inger-Lise, and Jonathan Hickman. 2013. Studying Fan Activities on Twitter: Reflections on Methodological Issues Emerging from a Case Study on the West Wing Fandom. *First Monday* 18 (9): np. http://dx.doi.org/10.5210/fm.v18i9.4268.

Lancaster, Kurt. 2001. *Interacting with Babylon 5: Fan Performances in a Media Universe*. Austin: University of Texas Press.
Lichterman, Joseph. 2017. This Site Is 'Taking the Edge Off Rant Mode' By Making Readers Pass a Quiz Before Commenting. *Nieman Lab*. http://www.niemanlab.org/2017/03/this-site-is-taking-the-edge-off-rant-mode-by-making-readers-pass-a-quiz-before-commenting/. Accessed 3 Mar.
Liu, Hugo. 2007. Social Network Profiles as Taste Performances. *Journal of Computer-Mediated Communication* 13 (1): 252–275.
Marcus, George E., W. Russell Neuman, and Michael MacKuen. 2000. *Affective Intelligence and Political Judgment*. Chicago: University of Chicago Press.
Marwick, Alice, Mary L. Gray, and Mike Ananny. 2014. "'Dolphins Are Just Gay Sharks'" Glee and the Queer Case of Transmedia as Text and Object. *Television & New Media* 15 (7): 627–647.
McKee, Alan. 2005. *The Public Sphere: An Introduction*. Cambridge: Cambridge University Press.
Papacharissi, Zizi. 2010. *A Networked Self: Identity, Community, and Culture on Social Network Sites*. New York/London: Routledge.
Probyn, Elspeth. 2005. *Blush: Faces of Shame*. Minneapolis: University of Minnesota Press.
Reich, Zvi. 2011. User Comments: The Transformation of Participatory Space. In *Participatory Journalism: Guarding Open Gates at Online Newspapers*, ed. Jane B. Singer, David Domingo, Ari Heinonen, Alfred Hermida, Steve Paulussen, Thorsten Quandt, Zvi Reich, and Marina Vujnovic, 96–117. West Sussex: Wiley.
Riley, Denise. 2005. *Impersonal Passion: Language as Affect*. Durham: Duke University Press.
Sandvoss, Cornel. 2005. *Fans: The Mirror of Consumption*. Cambridge: Polity.
Sedgwick, Eve Kosofsky and Adam Frank, (eds). 1995. *Shame and Its Sisters: A Silvan Tomkins Reader*. Durham: Duke University Press.
Seigworth, Gregory J., and Melissa Gregg. 2010. An Inventory of Shimmers. In *The Affect Theory Reader*, ed. Melissa Gregg and Gregory J. Seigworth, 1–28. Durham: Duke University Press.
Shepard, Alicia C. 2011. Online Comments: Dialogue or Diatribe? *Nieman Reports* 65 (2): 52–53.
Sherry, John L. 2004. Flow and Media Enjoyment. *Communication Theory* 14 (4): 328–347.
Singer, Jane B., and Ian Ashman. 2009. 'Comment Is Free, But Facts Are Sacred': User-Generated Content and Ethical Constructs at the Guardian. *Journal of Mass Media Ethics* 24 (1): 3–21.
Tomkins, Silvan S. 1995. *Exploring Affect: The Selected Writings of Silvan S. Tomkins*. Ed. Virginia E. Demos. Cambridge: Cambridge University Press.

Van Zoonen, Liesbet. 2005. *Entertaining The Citizen: When Politics and Popular Culture Converge.* Lanham: Rowman & Littlefield.

Veale, Kevin. 2013. Capital, Dialogue, and Community Engagement—My Little Pony: Friendship Is Magic Understood as an Alternate Reality Game. *Transformative Works and Cultures,* 14: np. http://journal.transformativeworks.org/index.php/twc/article/view/510/405.

Weber, Patrick. 2014. Discussions in the Comments Section: Factors Influencing Participation and Interactivity in Online Newspapers' Reader Comments. *New Media & Society* 16 (6): 941–957.

Wetherell, Margaret. 2012. *Affect and Emotion: A New Social Science Understanding.* Thousand Oaks: Sage Publications.

Wood, Megan M., and Linda Baughman. 2012. Glee Fandom and Twitter: Something New, or More of the Same Old Thing? *Communication Studies* 63 (3): 328–344.

CHAPTER 3

The Online/Offline Life

When we are online, we are also offline. Our choices of how, why, what and where to comment online are inextricable from the practices of our everyday lives. We may be checking our social media profiles while waiting in line at the supermarket or commenting on online news stories while watching television; our informational diets and repertoires of engagement need to be understood as being related to our offline activities. Therefore, to understand online commenting culture, we need to examine how our online interactions affect our other practices and vice versa.

The previous chapter drew on fan studies to show how an affective relationship with online content and other members of a virtual community can impact upon an individual's commenting behaviour. In the process, we viewed the diverse entities that are described as "media" as a text. As a text, media is something that can be analysed and interpreted by individuals or an audience.

In this chapter, we shift our focus and draw on sociologist and media scholar Nick Couldry (2004, 2014) to view media as a set of practices and determine how media usage is ordered, controlled and anchored by other social and cultural practices, and vice versa. Couldry (2014, p. 215) argues that the audience is the "domain of media-related practice outside production within specialist institutions". From this point of view, we can explore how our commenting behaviour is influenced by time, space, and institutional and individual constraints (Couldry 2014) or, put simply, how our offline world impacts upon our online one.

© The Author(s) 2018
R. Barnes, *Uncovering Online Commenting Culture*,
https://doi.org/10.1007/978-3-319-70235-3_3

This approach is in line with anthropologist S. Elizabeth Bird (2003) who has argued that too much focus is placed on the active contributors of media (those making comments, for instance) without taking into account the many varied ways that we can interact online and how this is impacted by our "everyday life":

> We cannot really isolate the role of media in culture, because the media are firmly anchored into the web of culture, although articulated by individuals in different ways ... The "audience" is "everywhere and nowhere". (2003, pp. 2–3)

Bird is posing two aspects that we need to consider, the role of media in our culture—which, to frame it within practice theory (Couldry 2014, 2004) would be considered a media-orientated practice—and everyday life, which would be viewed as constraints on time, space, and institutional and individual factors.

THE PRACTICE OF COMMENTING

To start, then, let us explore the media-orientated practices relevant to the online commenting culture. The practice of commenting could be seen as part of the larger practice of online information-seeking. Costera Meijer and Groot Kormelink's (2015) study of news usage provides a useful framework for understanding this categorisation. They identified 16 practices of news use: reading, watching, listening, viewing, checking, snacking, monitoring, scanning, searching, clicking, linking, sharing, liking, recommending, commenting and voting. Of these diverse media-orientated practices, some are visible and some are not, and none are media-platform specific. Instead, these practices relate to *how* individuals undertake news usage and how that practice is anchored to other activities within the everyday.

This approach is similar to the ones taken by other studies that have examined how news usage orders and even anchors other social and cultural practices (Schrøder 2014; Domingo et al. 2015). For example, the practices of reading and watching are associated with in-depth or intense concentration, while viewing or listening are more about "wallpapering" the day—practices undertaken while completing other activities such as preparing dinner or driving. Other activities such as checking, snacking, scanning or monitoring are also practices that relate to the availability of time and other situational or locational elements of an individual's day.

Likewise, clicking is linked to investment, as an additional activity on top of checking or snacking on news. Linking, sharing, liking, recommending, commenting and voting on news are practices that require more active investment and generate personal benefit through image management (Costera Meijer and Groot Kormelink 2015). Overall, the study suggests that audience news-usage encompasses a complex spectrum of practices influenced by motivational as well as time and space factors.

Also of note is that this spectrum of practice relates to a:

> broadening definition of what counts as news to users: not just events as described by journalists, but everything that is new: from the developments in the personal life of your Facebook friends, opinions on Twitter to information on specific websites within your field. (Costera Meijer and Groot Kormelink 2015, p. 676, *[sic]*)

Therefore, we can understand the practice of commenting, as well as the practices of checking, snacking, scanning, monitoring and reading of comments, as being linked to the larger practice of information-seeking. What, then, are the time, space, and institutional and individual constraints that will impact upon the practice of information-seeking?

TIME AND SPACE

Firstly, let us examine how time and space, which, broadly speaking, can be understood as the "when and where", impact upon our practice choices. The practice of writing a comment, along with liking, sharing, recommending and voting, was found to require more personal and emotional investment and, therefore, more dedicated time and space. This level of investment was due to the mindfulness applied to the impression that would be made by, and the reactions of others to, that comment (Costera Meijer and Groot Kormelink 2015). This reflects Picone's (2011) study of Flemish online-news users, which found that productive news-use or "produsage"—"correcting, evaluating, completing, marking ... or commenting on" news (2011, p. 99) is shaped by motivational, situational and social factors. Specifically, it found that users need to be in "the mood for produsage" and must be prepared to make the level of investment needed to actively contribute in one of these ways:

> [U]sers do not always feel like contributing. Especially when online news is used between times or to quickly catch up with the news, participants

seemed not willing to react extensively on it. Also work stress, domestic tasks, and other time-consuming activities shape a user's mood for produsage. (Picone 2011, p. 112)

The practice of checking requires less investment. Costera Meijer and Groot Kormelink (2015) found that the practice of checking, defined as a habitual activity of finding out if anything new has occurred, is associated with micro-moments, such as waiting for a red light or riding an elevator. They also noted it could be intertwined with an activity such as waking up in the morning, or with a social experience like having a drink.

Snacking is about getting a basic overview of information, not an in-depth knowledge or developed opinions, and is used as a diversion. It is more relaxed than checking, so therefore may involve more investment, and therefore more time, and it can be influenced by other factors such as distractions from social settings.

Scanning is different from checking and snacking in that it is focused on gathering highlights, or the overall gist, of what is going on. This is often used to provide a common ground with someone or to join conversations offline. It is a quick activity, often undertaken prior to a particular social event.

Monitoring is defined as "keeping an eye out, [and being] prepared to come into action when needed" (Costera Meijer and Groot Kormelink 2015, p. 671). This practice is associated with "push notifications" for applications on smartphones—for example, a notification from Facebook when a comment is made on a thread that you have previously commented on. In this way, the practice of monitoring is forced on the individual at a time and in a place that is not of his or her choosing.

Reading, however, is undertaken at a time and in a place of the individual's choosing. It is an in-depth pursuit requiring concentration, so it will be undertaken at a suitable time and in a place or space with minimal distractions.

These practices have been articulated in other ways. Crawford's (2009) study of Twitter users found that many undertake "background listening", in which they slip in and out of the "conversation" throughout the day. My own work (Barnes 2016) examined readers of alternative journalism websites and found both active contributors, who leave comments and other productive flags of participation, and "engaged listeners", who read these websites and the comments left by other users. All of these practices help the individual to form an affective relationship with the online community associated with that website.

What is key here is that, by categorising these practices, it is possible to see how one individual may undertake different practices, depending on time and space factors. When we have lots of time (for instance, while waiting in a doctor's surgery), we will choose to undertake a practice that requires more investment—we may read comments in depth and even comment ourselves. When we have less time, we may just check our social media accounts and not read in depth or take the time to comment.

Sometimes, time and space factors will combine to form a habit. As Couldry (2014, p. 221) notes:

> Habits involve not only simple acts of repetition, but also the regular linking together of whole bundles of actions as part of wider lifestyles and ways of coordinating work, family responsibilities, and leisure.

It is therefore a combination of time and space factors, as well as individual preferences (which will be discussed in more detail next), that influence our media practice. For example, we may habitually check Facebook before going to sleep each night, as this is when family responsibilities have been taken care of. This habit will influence the type and regularity of our practice.

Other studies have investigated the blurring of our online and offline lives by examining the impact of offline meetings among online community participants and found that participants of online communities who meet offline enhance their bonding social capital at the expense of their bridging social capital (Shen and Cage 2015; Sessions 2010). As outlined in Chap. 1, "bridging social capital" refers to weak ties that bind a disparate group and provides opportunities for access to diverse opinions and information. "Bonding social capital" relates to close connections, such as family and friends, or strong ties, and offers little diversity in information or opinions. The enhanced bonding capital felt by those who met offline can fragment the online community, as they can become less connected to other members in general (Sessions 2010). As bridging capital is necessary in terms of integrating new members, these offline meetings can then impact upon online behaviour, with members rigidly enforcing established community norms and not including other members (Shen and Cage 2015). Therefore, by physically meeting in the same time and space, the fundamental dynamics and therefore the types of practices undertaken by community members can change.

Overall, then, time and space factors will influence which media practices we undertake and embed them within the social and cultural practices of our everyday lives. What is happening offline will impact on our choice of media practice and, in the case of offline meetings, could influence our ongoing behaviour, as it will fundamentally change online group dynamics and interactions.

THE INSTITUTION AND THE INDIVIDUAL

Next, we will look at the institutional and individual factors that influence which practice we undertake. Institutional factors can be easily understood as the "how" (Couldry 2014). *How* are we undertaking the media practice, and what might be the constraints on this factor of our practice?

As noted above, checking and monitoring are associated with smartphone use, which can impact upon the time and place in which we undertake a practice, but a smartphone presents other constraints on practice. For example, it is possible to access the internet on a smartphone, but this access may be heavily constrained by cost and connection speed. Even the specific technological affordances of a platform, such as the ability to provide feedback to content in the form of a reply comment or rating, will influence what practice we undertake. Practices will be platform specific. If the option to comment or offer a rating is not provided, then we may alter our practice, quickly checking and snacking and moving on; however, if these options are offered, we may choose to engage more deeply, reading the comments so that we might react. Ling's (2012) analysis of the mobile phone as a device that is "taken for granted" in our everyday lives further informs the increasing role that the device used has in influencing our practice choice. He argues that our phones are so woven into the social fabric of our lives that we have changed our expectations about how our interpersonal relationships are conducted. We access social media on our phones (at all times and locations) to follow the ebb and flow of activity in our social sphere, but we have an expectation of reciprocity from the people in our networks. We expect that they are keeping abreast of updates and will respond accordingly.

Likewise, the user interface of a particular platform will differ between smartphones, tablets and desktop computers. User interfaces, or the method that we use to access a platform and also write a comment, can control the ease with which an individual might read, check, snack, scan or monitor a website (de Souza and Preece 2004). User interfaces will also influence the ease with which we can undertake the practice of commenting. For example, It may be far easier to leave a comment when accessing a platform on a desktop computer, but on a smartphone we may find it easier to rate a comment or Like it. Therefore, the institutional factor of the user interface will also influence our choice of media practice.

Hampton (2016) has further argued that the technological affordances of digital media, and of social networking sites in particular, have fundamentally changed our conception of community:

> As with many earlier technologies, digital communication technologies have reduced the costs of interacting across time and space. Yet recent technologies have also introduced widespread affordances of persistent contact and pervasive awareness that have the potential to fundamentally change the structure of community. (2016, p. 118)

This reconfiguration of what and who is within our "community" impacts upon how our media practice is embedded in our social life. For Hampton, social media and related technologies make available relational persistence and ambient interaction, which impact upon our everyday lives because how we behave online and, in particular, the social structures online impact upon our offline worlds. A status update or a comment on a post that might appear to be trivial, as well as those about "heavier" topics such as politics, health or finance, affords a "pervasive awareness" that provides for relational maintenance and stronger ties with others in our network. When we connect through a social networking site, social ties have the potential to be enduring communication channels. The broadcast nature of social networks enables contact to be maintained without the substantial time or resource commitments required by other forms of communication.

> You may never truly lose contact with friends, including those who are "unfriended" through social media and those who are never directly articulated, because awareness continues through mutual acquaintances and shared and persistent content. (Hampton 2016, p. 111)

Pervasive awareness may result if one is the recipient or initiator of communication because responses to updates provide an "awareness of others' awareness" (Hampton 2016, p. 113). Social networking sites, Hampton argues, differ from other advances in digital communication because they enable this persistent contact and pervasive awareness.

Hampton (2016) further argues that the ambient nature of technologies that enable pervasive awareness means that most individuals are passive recipients of information, akin to "lurkers", on other virtual platforms. Indeed, studies have shown that only a small percentage of people who access online forums actively contribute (Brandtzæg 2012; van Dijck 2009; Ling et al. 2005). However, while an individual may not leave a flag of participation online, he or she could still be acting on that information at a later date offline. For example, an individual may notice a status update sharing a photograph of a meal at a restaurant, which leads him or her to discuss that restaurant with a colleague at work or even make a booking there. Equally, he or she may be made aware of a friend of a friend who has died tragically of heart disease, which motivates him or her to have a health checkup.

The persistent contact and pervasive awareness offered by the technological affordances of social media can also serve to initiate collective action. Many studies have already shown the role of social media in collective action and its ability to reveal when an action reaches critical mass, thereby motivating more individuals to join—for example, the political action of the Arab Spring (Papacharissi 2015; Hussain and Howard 2013; Tufekci and Wilson 2012). Other scholars have argued that an awareness through social media of the political opinions of others in our network could inspire a "spiral of silence", whereby individuals will self-censor if they do not share those opinions (Scheufle and Moy 2000). This self-censoring may occur both in online and offline discussions (Hampton et al. 2014).

The technological affordances created by the institutions that own the platforms on which we comment, therefore, will impact upon our choice of practice as well as how our media practice controls, anchors and orders our other social and cultural practices.

There are also individual constraints, such as technical skills, which impact upon our media practice. If, as outlined above, individuals commenting do so as a form of self-presentation (Costera Meijer and Groot Kormelink 2015), then the confidence and technical skills to present oneself in a particular way will also impact upon the media practice chosen. Social media users have been found to suffer online if their technical skills are not adequate for managing their online presence (Litt and Hargittai

2014), while Picone's (2011) study of news users found that if an individual felt that his or her writing was poor or his or her augmentative skills were lacking, then he or she would not comment, being worried about the reaction of others.

But just who are the "others" that will react to a comment? Who is our audience when we are commenting online? These questions are referred to as the "audience problem" of online commenting culture (Hampton 2016) and put another individual constraint on our media practice. Users must not only have the technical and writing skills to make a comment, but also have the skills to perceive who the audience is that will read, check, snack, scan or monitor that comment.

THE AUDIENCE PROBLEM

This imagined audience is a "mental conceptualisation of the people with whom we are communicating" (Litt 2012, p. 331) and is what we use as a guide for what is appropriate and relevant to share when the actual audience is not physically present or is unknown. The imagined audience presents a particular problem for online interactions, particularly those on social media, as users can suffer from a "context collapse" (Marwick and boyd 2011; boyd 2008), in which they interact with and broadcast to large and diverse audiences. In face-to-face interactions, we typically interact with small, explicit audiences. However, the online platforms in which we interact alter the size, composition, boundaries and accessibility of these audiences, making it nearly impossible to determine our actual audiences (Litt 2012). According to the theory of self-presentation, to help control the impressions that others form of us, we interact and adapt our behaviour based on our audience (Goffman 1959). When we are offline, we rely on whatever limited cues are provided by our audience, such as tone of voice or physical reactions (Goffman 1959), to make these adaptations. But what happens when the audience is unknown or difficult to determine, and we are not provided with the cues needed to appropriately adapt our behaviour? This question forms another individual constraint.

Hogan (2010) has argued that what results is an identity performance that is appropriate to the potential multiple audiences (for example, work colleagues, family members and distant friends). Therefore, for those of us who are (or able to be) conscious of these multiple audiences, our commenting behaviour will represent selective self-presentation that we deem appropriate for the strong, weak and latent ties networked through that

platform. Other scholars, however, have found a more disturbing disconnect between the actual and imagined audiences, with the consequences
described as embarrassment, the revelation of previously hidden information, or simply audience disinterest (boyd 2010; Davis and Jurgenson
2014). Additionally, in comparison to offline interactions, online communication tends to be more persistent, searchable, archiveable and shareable
(boyd 2010; Quinn 2014), making a faux pas potentially everlasting. A
comment or status update that is a complaint about an employer, for
example, could potentially be found by a future employer many years later.

Litt and Hargittai (2016) examined users of Facebook and Twitter and
found that, even though users often interacted with large and diverse audiences when they posted, they were actually envisioning either abstract,
imagined audiences or more targeted, specific imagined audiences. About
half of the time when posting, participants imagined an abstract audience
or not anyone specifically. This reflects other studies in which Twitter users
suggested the "public" or a "broad audience of disparate tastes" was reading their tweets (Marwick and boyd 2011, pp. 120–121), and those sharing photographs on Facebook envisaged a "generalised audience of the
Internet" (Cook and Teasley 2011, p. 44).

These broad, abstract imaginings of the audience would suggest that
content shared would be less likely to be offensive, as it would be deemed
appropriate for a diverse range of people. However, just under 50% of the
time, study participants were imagining a more targeted audience, which
the authors divided into the categories of personal ties, communal ties,
professional ties and phantasmal ties (Litt and Hargittai 2016). Personal
ties were the most imagined targeted audience and consisted of close
friends and family. Communal ties were the next-most-imagined targeted
audience and were those from a specific community—for example, a specific geographic community ("anyone based in Portland"), or a community of people with particular shared hobbies or experiences ("everyone
with kids") or ideologies ("Christians") (2016, p. 6). At other times, users
imagined professional ties such as co-workers or potential employers and
even phantasmal ties, which are those "with whom they had an illusionary
relationship such as famous individuals, brands, animals and the deceased"
(2016, p. 6). Overall, Litt and Hargittai's (2016) study found that people's imagined audiences fluctuated. While there were times when having
abstract imagined audiences mitigated against trouble from potentially
broad and diverse actual audiences, the times when people had imagined
targeted and specific audiences also had the potential to create disharmony,

as the imagined audience did not necessarily align with the actual audience. Obviously, problems will arise in terms of harmonious, effective and inclusive online communities if there is a disconnect between the audience imagined when a comment is typed and the audience actually reading, checking, snacking, scanning or monitoring the comment. The person writing the comment might suffer reputational consequences and embarrassment (as outlined above), but the larger online community will suffer because different audiences may have different expectations of appropriateness and relevance.

Given that problems arise when there is a disconnect between who we imagine to be our audience and the actual audience, it is important to understand the factors or cues that we use online that help us imagine who is engaging with our comments. Feedback in the form of a reply comment or a Like demonstrates an awareness or attention from particular audience-members, with many Facebook users envisaging those who they interact with most as their imagined audience (Strater and Lipford 2008). Bloggers have also been shown to identify their most active commenters as their imagined audience (Stern 2008). The feedback of a comment or Like then plays a vital role in our online behaviour, as the audience problem is not just about the possibility of multiple audiences, but is also "the result of an inability to gauge interest and attention to content" posted (Hampton 2016, p. 113). Therefore, the feedback of a comment or Like gives us an indication of not only who makes up the audience of the content posted, but also the level of interest in that particular content. However, this feedback can create an artificial sense of confidence in the composition and interest of our imagined audience. Just because a close friend or family member has liked a particularly divisive or politically partisan post that you have made, does not mean that those who are potentially offended by the post are not reading it.

Rating systems or binary thumbs-up or thumbs-down are measures that many platforms have introduced to help regulate the quality of commentary. However, studies have shown that these measures have a limited impact as far as reducing hostile or unhelpful comments. In Sierodorfer, Chelaru, Nejdl and Pedro's (2010) analysis of comment rating through the thumbs-up and thumbs-down binary on YouTube, they found that the community casts more positive than negative votes, and that most comments were either not rated by other users or evaluated neutrally. Likewise, less than half of the reviews on Amazon were rated by other users for their helpfulness (Kim et al. 2006). The lack of use of these

systems has been attributed to a disconnect between the perceived benefit
of a rating and the cost to make one. Users pay for each rating in terms of
mental effort, time and the potential for a negative reaction, but have the
potential benefits of fun, more accurate recommendations and increased
social capital. Users will only provide a rating if the benefit outweighs the
cost (Sparling and Sen 2011, p. 149). So, while platforms can put in measures to help create cues for socially acceptable behaviours, these still may
not accurately reflect "the audience" and therefore "appropriate" behaviour still relies on the individual having the will and ability to provide that
feedback.

Our frequent offline interactions also play a role in the development of
our imagined audience, and that audience is most likely to include people
"drawn from the accessible environment" who are "likely to resemble the
last strong character we have been in contact with" (Cooley 1902,
pp. 59–60 cited in Litt 2012). Feedback then gathered on- and offline
from, for example, friends, family and co-workers, will help us determine
our imagined audience online. The social norms that we are exposed to,
then, will be influential, as they will be used to determine who we "should"
be imagining as our audience. However, this still presents an issue in terms
of representing the actual audience.

HIGH AND LOW SELF-MONITORING INDIVIDUALS

Some individuals may also have a greater motivation and/or ability to
perceive the appropriateness of content than others, regardless of feedback. Litt (2012) uses Snyder's (1974) concept of high and low self-
monitors to determine how particular individuals might interpret
online social cues and how this impacts upon the imagining of the
audience online. Snyder (1974) outlines a high self-monitor as someone who is sensitive to and motivated by external social cues such as
status, moods and norms. By comparison, low self-monitors are less
attuned to context and are more likely to act based on internal dispositions and personal beliefs, rather than perceived social cues. People
who are high self-monitors are more attuned to online social norms
and online or offline contextual clues, and are therefore better at per-
ceiving the actual audience of content posted. Low self-monitors, who
are less concerned with social desirability, lack the motivation or ability
to interpret clues provided in the online environment. For these
individuals,

[t]heir imagined audience might be a fictionalized ideal group of like-minded individuals, fans or even themselves. (Litt 2012, p. 338)

Therefore, those who are not particularly motivated or able to pick up social cues offline are just as unlikely to do so online.

However, there are additional difficulties with ascertaining who is accessing our content online and when they are doing so, due to techno-logical structures and affordances, which are partially responsible for limit-ing and exposing clues about our actual audience. Take, for instance, the privacy settings available on particular platforms. Facebook provides the ability to make lists so that we can limit content to specific groups, which, if used, means we are more likely to correctly imagine our actual audience. Content we share on Twitter or following an online news article, however, is broadcast to all our followers (in the case of Twitter) and all readers (in the case of a news website), so there is no affordance for directing appro-priate communication to a specific group. Litt (2012) argues that high self-monitors will be more likely to utilise privacy settings, when available, and adapt content to suit a broad audience spectrum when these affor-dances are not available. However, it could also be argued that high self-monitors would be less likely to use a "thumbs-down" or negative-rating approach, as this could reflect aggressive social behaviour. Dillard (1990) has argued that high-self monitors desire to manage their self-presentation while successfully avoiding loss of face by themselves as well as those they are communicating with. High self-monitors, then, will be more likely to communicate "appropriate" content, but will be less likely to intervene when others are hostile or uncivil, and thereby establish normative com-munity values that encourage harmonious interactions.

ALGORITHMS AS SOCIAL CONVENORS

Difficulties identifying our actual audiences online are intensified for even the most attuned and motivated by affordances that are beyond an indi-vidual's control. Each platform on which we make our comments utilises different curators or algorithms that mediate the why, when, how and who of our posted content (Hogan 2010). Facebook, for example, uses an algorithm to determine in which of an individual's contacts' newsfeeds a post will appear. Someone might read that post immediately, but, given the permanence and archivability of content (Hampton 2010; boyd 2010), someone else may access that same content months later, when looking through the individual's timeline. Twitter also uses an algorithm to over-ride its real-time newsfeed and determine which posts will appear in its "In case you missed it" section. Sometimes it is an individual curator who will influence the actual audience. Many news organisations and specialist forums use moderators to highlight particular comments, in an attempt to ensure a more robust and quality debate. The online environments in which we are posting our comments, then, "fundamentally obscure actual audience members", and "such conditions may provide or entice individuals who tend to, or even wish to, ignore the real audience" (Litt 2012, p. 339). These affordances are institutional constraints, but also operate as individual constraints, influencing our media practice and potentially invigorating more inappropriate content to be shared online than in the offline world.

However, it is not just curation or algorithms that enhance the context collapse of the imagined audience. Implicit norms about who uses the site will influence how we think about our audience. For example, policies around the use of real names or pseudonyms will impact upon how the audience is imagined. The use of real names may enable a more accurate and specific imagining, while the use of pseudonyms may limit the cues available to determine the actual audience. Anonymity has been shown to increase hostile and uncivil comments (Meyer and Carey 2014), which suggests that a potential impact is an inaccurately imagined audience. The provision of analytical tools, or websites that provide visible data on who visits a site, however, may have the potential to help us configure a more accurate imagining of the audience.

Overall, then, the technological and structural affordances of the platforms and interfaces we use to make comments will impact on not only the type of media practice we undertake (as outlined earlier) but also the appropriateness of our commenting behaviour, due to the influences they have on our imaginings of the audiences engaging with the content we post. The individual constraints of our technical skills as well as our skill and motivation to perceive our actual audience will also impact upon our media practice.

Conclusion: The Online/Offline Nexus

In viewing commenting as a media-orientated practice, it becomes necessary to understand it as embedded in social life (Ruddock 2007). As Couldry (2014) notes, this approach enables us to understand the social consequences of our actions as well as the particular constraints that influence them. Overall, commenting is part of the larger practice of information-seeking. The writing of a comment is also part of a larger network of practices surrounding the reception of the comment, including the practices of checking, snacking, scanning, monitoring and reading of comments.

These media-orientated practices are embedded in our everyday lives and are therefore influenced and constrained by time and space factors. When and where we log online will influence our choice of practice. There will be occasions where we have more time to invest and will choose our practice accordingly. Likewise, where we happen to be at the time of logging on will also impact on our practice. These temporal and spatial influences mean that our online interactions cannot be assessed as distinct from our offline lives.

Likewise, there are institutional and individual constraints that influence our practice. The institutions that own and develop the devices and platforms through and on which we comment have an enormous influence over the structural and technological factors that influence our online interactions. The technological affordances of the online platforms on which we comment will not only influence the ease with which we interact with a community (either constraining or enhancing our experience), but also fundamentally reconfigure that community. Our community (which is the epicentre of our interactions) does not vastly modify and adapt as we move through life (for example, leave school, move town or change jobs), as we can retain persistent contact with its members. Likewise, social media in particular enables a pervasive awareness that provides a closeness and information exchange, which continually informs our on- and offline interactions (Hampton 2016).

These structural and technological affordances are closely linked to an individual's constraints. An individual's practice will be impacted by his or her skill, both in writing a comment and in using the interfaces provided.

The constraints of individuals are further complicated by our motivations and abilities to perceive the audiences of our contributions, or "the audience problem". We learn to socialise offline based on visual and verbal cues given by the people we are interacting with. When we move those social interactions to an online space, where those cues are either removed or obscured, a fundamental component of how we moderate our own behaviour is also eliminated. Without the availability of social cues to determine who is paying attention, it is difficult to determine the appropriateness of content. Feedback from others online and people we associate with offline can influence how we imagine our audience when writing a comment, but this imagined audience could be vastly different from the diverse actual audience that is enabled through persistent contact online (whose practice is in turn influenced by each member's own time and space factors). Additionally, there are hidden factors such as algorithms and curators that will further obscure the actual audience.

Overall, then, the media-orientated practice of commenting intersects with other social and cultural practices and is heavily influenced by time, space, and institutional and individual constraints.

Examining commenting in this way provides a method of understanding how we can influence online commenting culture. As individuals, we need to be aware of the potential audience problem and adjust our behaviour accordingly. Education may be necessary not only in the use of technology, to make undertaking our practice easy, but also in constructing a realistic imagined audience. This may involve learning strategies to gain more insight into the make-up of the potential audience, such as using a site's analytics functionality or taking greater control of privacy settings. The institutions that develop the devices and the platforms also have a responsibility to help us manage our online performance—for example, by providing more tools that bring awareness of the actual audience through cues, reminders or enhancing privacy settings. Overall, these tools will not only empower individuals to take more control, but can help them create the harmonious and inclusive spaces for interaction that they desire.

The next chapter will further examine the intersection of individual and institutional responsibilities in creating an ideal commenting culture by examining the role of individual difference, or personality, in commenting behaviour and how technological affordances and policies can influence the types of individuals who will contribute.

REFERENCES

Barnes, Renee. 2016. The Ecology of Participation. In *The SAGE Handbook of Digital Journalism*, ed. Tamara Witschge, Chris Anderson, David Domingo, and Alfred Hermida, 179–191. New York: Sage.

Bird, S. Elizabeth. 2003. *The Audience in Everyday Life: Living in a Media World*. London: Routledge.

boyd, Danah. 2008. *Taken Out of Context: American Teen Sociality in Networked Publics*. Berkeley: University of California.

————. 2010. Social Network Sites as Networked Publics: Affordances, Dynamics, and Implications. In *A Networked Self: Identity, Community, and Culture on Social Network Sites*, ed. Zizi Papacharissi, 9–58. New York: Routledge.

Brandtzæg, Petter Bae. 2012. Social Networking Sites: Their Users and Social Implications—A Longitudinal Study. *Journal of Computer-Mediated Communication* 17 (4): 467–488. https://doi.org/10.1111/j.1083-6101.2012.01580.x.

Cook, Eric C., and Stephanie D. Teasley. 2011. *Beyond Promotion and Protection: Creators, Audiences and Common Ground in User-Generated Media*. Proceedings of the 2011 iConference, Seattle, February.

Costera Meijer, Irene, and Tim Groot Kormelink. 2015. Checking, Sharing, Clicking and Linking: Changing Patterns of News Use Between 2004 and 2014. *Digital Journalism* 3 (5): 664–679.

Couldry, Nick. 2004. Theorising Media as Practice. *Social Semiotics* 14 (2): 115–132.

————. 2014. The Necessary Future of the Audience … and How to Research It. In *The Handbook of Media Audiences*, ed. Virginia Nightingale, 213–229. Chichester: Wiley.

Crawford, Kate. 2009. Following You: Disciplines of Listening in Social Media. *Continuum: Journal of Media & Cultural Studies* 23 (4): 525–535.

Davis, Jenny L., and Nathan Jurgenson. 2014. Context Collapse: Theorizing Context Collusions and Collisions. *Information, Communication & Society* 17 (4): 476–485.

De Souza, Clarisse Sieckenius, and Jenny Preece. 2004. A Framework for Analyzing and Understanding Online Communities. *Interacting with Computers* 16 (3): 579–610.

Dillard, James Price. 1990. A Goal-Driven Model of Interpersonal Influence. In *Seeking Compliance: The Production of Interpersonal Influence Messages*, ed. James Price Dillard, 41–56. Scottsdale: Gorsuch Scarisbrick.

Domingo, David, Pere Masip, and Irene Costera Meijer. 2015. Tracing Digital News Networks: Towards an Integrated Framework of the Dynamics of News Production, Circulation and Use. *Digital Journalism* 3 (1): 53–67.

Goffman, Erving. 1959. *The Presentation of Self in Everyday Life*. Garden City: Doubleday.

Hampton, Keith N. 2016. Persistent and Pervasive Community: New Communication Technologies and the Future of Community. *American Behavioral Scientist* 60 (1): 101–124.

Hampton, Keith N., Lee Rainie, Weixu Lu, Maria Dwyer, Inyoung Shin, and Kristen Purcell. 2014. *Social Media and the 'Spiral of Silence'*. Washington, DC: Pew Research Center. http://www.pewinternet.org/files/2014/08/PI_Social-networks-and-debate_082614.pdf.

Hogan, Bernie. 2010. The Presentation of Self in the Age of Social Media: Distinguishing Performances and Exhibitions Online. *Bulletin of Science, Technology & Society.* https://doi.org/10.1177/0270467610385893.

Hussain, Muzammil M., and Philip N. Howard. 2013. What Best Explains Successful Protest Cascades? ICTs and the Fuzzy Causes of the Arab Spring. *International Studies Review* 15 (1): 48–66.

Kim, Soo-Min, Patrick Pantel, Tim Chklovski, and Marco Pennacchiotti. 2006. *Automatically Assessing Review Helpfulness.* Proceedings of the 2006 Conference on Empirical Methods in Natural Language Processing, Sydney.

Ling, Richard. 2012. *Taken for Grantedness: The Embedding of Mobile Communication into Society.* Cambridge, MA/London: MIT Press.

Ling, Kimberly, Gerard Beenen, Pamela Ludford, Xiaoqing Wang, Klarissa Chang, Xin Li, Dan Cosley, Dan Frankowski, Loren Terveen, and Mamunur Rashid Al. 2005. Using Social Psychology to Motivate Contributions to Online Communities. *Journal of Computer-Mediated Communication* 10 (4): Article 10. https://doi.org/10.1111/j.1083-6101.2005.tb00273.x.

Litt, Eden. 2012. Knock, Knock. Who's There? The Imagined Audience. *Journal of Broadcasting & Electronic Media* 56 (3): 330–345.

Litt, Eden, and Eszter Hargittai. 2014. A Bumpy Ride on the Information Superhighway: Exploring Turbulence Online. *Computers in Human Behavior* 36: 520–529.

———. 2016. The Imagined Audience on Social Network Sites. *Social Media & Society* 2 (1). https://doi.org/10.1177/2056305116633482.

Marwick, Alice E., and Danah boyd. 2011. I Tweet Honestly, I Tweet Passionately: Twitter Users, Context Collapse, and the Imagined Audience. *New Media & Society* 13 (1): 114–133.

Meyer, Hans K., and Michael Clay Carey. 2014. In Moderation: Examining How Journalists' Attitudes Toward Online Comments Affect the Creation of Community. *Journalism Practice* 8 (2): 213–228.

Papacharissi, Zizi. 2015. *Affective Publics: Sentiment, Technology, and Politics.* Oxford: Oxford University Press.

Picone, Ike. 2011. Produsage as a Form of Self-Publication. A Qualitative Study of Casual News Produsage. *New Review of Hypermedia and Multimedia* 17 (1): 99–120.

Quinn, Kelly. 2014. An Ecological Approach to Privacy: 'Doing' Online Privacy at Midlife. *Journal of Broadcasting & Electronic Media* 58 (4): 562–580.

Ruddock, Andy. 2007. *Investigating Audiences.* London: Sage.

Scheufle, Dietram A., and Patricia Moy. 2000. Twenty-Five Years of the Spiral of Silence: A Conceptual Review and Empirical Outlook. *International Journal of Public Opinion Research* 12 (1): 3–28.

Schrøder, Kim Christian. 2014. News Media Old and New: Fluctuating Audiences, News Repertoires and Locations of Consumption. *Journalism Studies* 16 (1): 60–78.

Sessions, Lauren F. 2010. How Offline Gatherings Affect Online Communities: When Virtual Community Members 'Meetup'. *Information, Communication & Society* 13 (3): 375–395.

Shen, Cuihua, and Charles Cage. 2015. Exodus to the Real World? Assessing the Impact of Offline Meetups on Community Participation and Social Capital. *New Media & Society* 17 (3): 394–414.

Siersdorfer, Stefan, Sergiu Chelaru, Wolfgang Nejdl, and Jose San Pedro. 2010. *How Useful Are Your Comments?: Analyzing and Predicting YouTube Comments and Comment Ratings*. Proceedings of the 19th International Conference on World Wide Web, Raleigh.

Snyder, Mark. 1974. Self-Monitoring of Expressive Behavior. *Journal of Personality and Social Psychology* 30 (4): 526.

Sparling, E. Isaac, and Shilad Sen. 2011. *Rating: How Difficult Is It?* Proceedings of the Fifth ACM Conference on Recommender Systems, Chicago, October 23–27.

Stern, Susannah. 2008. Producing Sites, Exploring Identities: Youth Online Authorship. In *Youth, Identity, and Digital Media*, ed. D. Buckingham, 95–118. Cambridge, MA: MIT Press.

Strater, Katherine, and Heather Richter Lipford. 2008. *Strategies and Struggles with Privacy in an Online Social Networking Community*. Proceedings of the 22nd British HCI Group Annual Conference on People and Computers: Culture, Creativity, Interaction-Volume 1, Swinton.

Tufekci, Zeynep, and Christopher Wilson. 2012. Social Media and the Decision to Participate in Political Protest: Observations from Tahrir Square. *Journal of Communication* 62 (2): 363–379.

van Dijck, José. 2009. Users Like You? Theorizing Agency in User-Generated Content. *Media, Culture & Society* 31 (1): 41–58.

CHAPTER 4

A Neurotic Extravert with a Pinch of Conscientiousness? How Personality Informs Commenting Behaviours

Defining the human character, our individual differences and how they impact on our behaviour has occupied scholars for at least 3000 years— Plato's book *The Republic* is interpreted by many psychologists as being one of the first discussions of the dimensions of personality. In the age of online media, the study of personality still offers much towards understanding how and why we behave the way we do. Just as our emotional engagement and specific socio-cultural circumstances (as outlined in the previous two chapters) can influence how we conduct ourselves online, so too can our personality traits. Additionally, understanding the role of personality in online behaviour sheds light on how the technological affordances and moderation policies of the online commenting environment influence particular individuals in their commenting practices.

Accordingly, this chapter will explore the relationships between personality, online commenting and the institutional factors of user interfaces and moderation policies. In doing so, it will outline some of the specific measures the institutions that control commenting platforms can take to mitigate "anti-social" commenting behaviour through specific moderation policies and modifications to user interfaces.

BIG FIVE PERSONALITY TRAITS

The study of personality within the broad field of psychology is the study of individual differences. Although different personality theorists have used different terms to describe the important dimensions of personality, it is possible to organise these dimensions in terms of five broad traits of personality. These are referred to as the Big Five Inventory (BFI) or Five Factor Model and are related to a set of continuums: Extraversion versus Introversion, Agreeableness versus Disagreeableness, Neuroticism versus Emotional Stability, Conscientiousness versus Disorganised and Openness to New Experiences versus Closed-mindedness (Costa and McCrae 1992). Interestingly, personality traits are enduring dispositions, (Roberts and DelVecchio 2000), meaning we do not change much as we age. However, most people will tend to decline in Neuroticism, Extraversion, and Openness to New Experiences, and to increase in Agreeableness and Closed-mindedness, throughout adulthood (McCrae and Costa 2003). There are small variations across gender, with women rating themselves consistently higher in Agreeableness and Neuroticism (Williams and Best 1990). The Five Factor Model has also been found to be universal across cultures (Terracciano and McCrae 2006), with the same psychological constructs found in cultures as diverse as Argentina, Iran, Malaysia, New Zealand, and Zimbabwe. Specifically, analysis of data from 51 cultures found a 95% variation within cultures and only about 5% across cultures (McCrae and Terracciano 2008), suggesting that culture, ethnicity and language have limited influence on personality traits. Australians and New Zealanders, Burkinabé and Batswana, Germans and Austrians, Americans and Canadians, and Hong Kong and Taiwan Chinese have similar profiles. Asian and African cultures tend to be similar and slightly different from Europeans and Americans, with higher scores in Extraversion for Europeans and Americans compared to Asian and African cultures (Terracciano and McCrae 2006). There was also limited variation in gender difference across cultures (Terracciano and McCrae 2006). Overall, then, the Five Factor Model is a reliable method of providing an analysis of individuals' behaviour regardless of age, gender or culture.

People who score high in Extraversion are characterised as outgoing, sociable, upbeat, friendly, assertive and gregarious. Typically, these individuals are depicted as the life and soul of the party, having engaging social skills and frequently drawing on humour and playfulness. Those who score low in this trait, Introverts, tend to be quiet and reflective, and prefer solitary situations (Costa and McCrae 1992).

Neuroticism presents as a lack of emotional adjustment and resilience when under stress. Individuals who score high in neuroticism are anxious, insecure, sensitive to ridicule, hostile, self-conscious and vulnerable (Costa and McCrae 1992). They are also inclined to pay more attention to negative events (Heller et al. 2002). People who are emotionally stable tend to be calm and less reactive (Costa and McCrae 1992).

Openness to New Experiences is associated with an individual's receptivity to learning, novelty and change (McCrae and John 1992). Someone who reflects a high level of Openness to New Experiences will be curious and creative, and seek novel experiences. Individuals who rate low in Openness to New Experiences are more likely to adhere to convention and established patterns (John and Srivastava 1999). A person low in Openness, or a closed-minded person, will not like his or her existing ideas challenged.

People who score high in Agreeableness are characterised as being sympathetic, trusting, cooperative, modest and straightforward. They have a preference for co-operation rather than competition, and tend to avoid conflict in social interactions. They tend to be associated with kindness and gratitude. Those who score low in Agreeableness (in other words, are Disagreeable) are less concerned with the well-being of others and have less empathy (Tan and Yang 2014).

Conscientiousness refers to people who are disciplined, diligent, dependable, detail-oriented, thorough, persistent and like to plan ahead (Ross et al. 2009). This trait relates to how individuals control their impulses, and individuals who score low in Conscientiousness (are Disorganised) prefer spontaneity to structured or planned activities (Costa and McCrae 1992).

Although the Five Factor Model does not account for all the nuances of human individuality, it has been successfully applied to many different areas of research and is particularly useful because it integrates a wide range of personality traits. Drawing on the work within this field makes it possible to determine why particular individuals engage online. Further, more recent studies have examined how personality relates to general activity online as well as specifically to activity on social media and in other online communities.

By drawing on the Five Factor Model, then, we can enhance our understanding of the participatory culture of commenting. In particular, the model helps us address questions such as, "Which individuals will leave particular types of comments?", "Who are the individuals making hostile and anti-social comments in our online communities?" and "How can we encourage people more likely to engage in civil conversation to take part in our online communities?"

PERSONALITY AND MOTIVATIONS FOR ONLINE ENGAGEMENT

Research suggests that personality traits are associated with the motivation for online engagement as well as the type of online behaviour exhibited. For example, Extraverts thrive on human interaction and are therefore largely motivated to use the internet as a means to seek, maintain and enhance their friendships and relationships with others (Cullen and Morse 2011; Orchard and Fullwood 2010; Ross et al. 2009). Extraverts are also motivated to engage in online activity to seek information and communicate about political matters, as the internet offers interesting discussion topics, interaction with others and a platform to voice their opinions (Amiel and Sargent 2004; Gerber et al. 2011).

In contrast, individuals high in Neuroticism have been found to spend extensive time on the internet largely to gain a sense of belonging, for social support and to stay informed (Amiel and Sargent 2004; Cullen and Morse 2011; Hamburger and Ben-Artzi 2000). Cullen and Morse (2011) found that, while individuals high in Neuroticism were under-represented in *active* online community engagement, 75% of those who participated identified that they did so to find a sense of belonging. Interestingly, individuals high in Neuroticism do not tend to use tools such as instant messaging or engage in group discussion, which could facilitate a greater sense of belonging. This is possibly due to the high levels of anxiety and apprehension associated with this personality trait and the need to avoid criticism or confrontations from other members (Amiel and Sargent 2004).

Highly Open individuals revel in new online technologies (McElroy et al. 2007) and tend to use the internet as a platform to gain new insights by tapping into the great variety of information and services online (Tuten and Bosnjak 2001). For example, Jadin et al. (2013) found that knowledge-sharing on Wikipedia was mostly influenced by trendsetting, a trait closely associated with Openness to Experience.

In regard to Agreeableness, the few studies conducted to date have yielded inconsistent findings. While individuals high in Agreeableness do perceive new technology as useful (Devaraj et al. 2008), general internet usage correlates negatively with a high level of Agreeableness (Andreassen et al. 2013; Landers and Lounsbury 2006). Further, although Agreeableness has been positively linked to news consumption (Gerber et al. 2011), suggesting that people high in this trait may use the internet to stay up-to-date on current political events, Russo and Amnå (2016) found a negative correlation between Agreeableness and informational use of the internet. This is most likely due to the lack of anonymity associated with some online activity, which could lead to conflict arising from criticism or disputes (Quintelier and Theocharis 2013; Russo and Amnå 2016). Supporting this notion, people who comment most frequently on news stories were found to be Disagreeable men (Barnes et al. forthcoming). That being so, highly Agreeable individuals might avoid the internet or certain online sites where there is high visibility, to avoid anti-social behaviours that cause disharmony or conflict with others.

Individuals high in Conscientiousness are likely to spend less time on the internet and therefore less time engaging in social networking behaviours (Buckels et al. 2014; Ross et al. 2009). However, Conscientious individuals are more willing to engage in an online community if it allows them to advance their work performance or has some personal benefit. Indeed, Conscientiousness has been positively related to searching for information (but not of a political nature), communicating with friends online (Hughes et al. 2012; Russo and Amnå 2016), pursuing academic study or sharing information (Landers and Lounsbury 2006; Matzler et al. 2008). Cullen and Morse (2011) found that individuals high in Conscientiousness who participated in online communities reported doing so to gain useful information and to give their opinion. However, when participants were spilt according to gender, only 41% of women were motivated by opinion-sharing while 67% liked to provide information and 86% felt they received useful information. In contrast, 80% of men were motivated by sharing their opinion. This suggests that gender is an important point of difference in that women high in Conscientiousness are motivated by the sharing of useful information, whereas Conscientious men are motivated by the sharing of opinions.

We can conclude, then, that our personalities can influence our motivations to engage in an online community. Delving deeper, it also becomes clear that personality is linked to how we behave in these online communities.

PERSONALITY AND PARTICIPATORY BEHAVIOURS

Despite the growing popularity of online communities (see Chap. 1 for an overview of these communities), research suggests that only a small percentage are active contributors (Brandtzæg 2012; van Dijck 2009; Ling et al. 2005). A number of factors have been linked to why individuals join and participate in online communities, including receiving social support

(Blanchard and Markus 2002), information exchange (Ridings and Gefen 2004) and a shared emotional connection (Barnes 2014; Blanchard and Markus 2002). Importantly, personality traits also appear to impact on who chooses to become a member of and participate in an online community (Devaraj et al. 2008).

Social media such as Facebook, LinkedIn and Twitter rely, at least in part, on the existing offline relationships of individuals. Ross et al. (2009) looked at Facebook use and found that, while individuals high in Extraversion belonged to more Facebook groups than Introverts, they did not have more friends and did not engage in more communication than those low in Extraversion. Further, Blau and Barak (2012) found a significant interaction between Extraversion and communication mode, such that Extraverts preferred taking part via more revealing communication mediums (for example, spoken, face-to-face discussions), whereas Introverts preferred holding discussions via text chat. Similarly, Cullen and Morse (2011) reported that Extraverts who actively participated in online communities did so out of a sense of friendship. However, when gender was included as a moderating factor, only 25% of men, but 80% of women, considered friendship a key factor in their joining an online community (Cullen and Morse 2011). These findings suggest that individuals who are more satisfied with their outward social life (in other words, highly Extraverted) use social media as a tool to strengthen and maintain ties to their offline groups, but not as an alternative to social activities. Introverts, however, may use online communication as a substitute for offline communication.

Individuals high in Neuroticism value online communal activities that foster relationships and social support (Amiel and Sargent 2004; Realo et al. 2011), and they are more likely to use online outlets such as blogging (Guadagno et al. 2008), social media (Correa et al. 2010) and chat rooms (Anolli et al. 2005) to express their opinions. Online social interaction is different from face-to-face interaction in that it offers both anonymity (for example, friendships may be formed without physical presence and proximity) and gives the user far greater control (for example, the ability to choose when to log on or off, and edit or re-write). According to McKenna and Bargh (2000), people are driven to interact online by self-related and social-related motives. Individuals who find it hard to meet their self-related needs in the immediate environment due to personality constraints (for example, being highly anxious or reserved—a typical Neurotic individual) will seek to find an alternative social environment where their "real me"—that is, their personality and needs—can be fully expressed. Whereas Extraverts and Emotionally Stable individuals locate their "real me" in traditional offline social interaction, Introverted and Neurotic individuals locate their "real me" on the internet (Amichai-Hamburger et al. 2002). This may explain why individuals who are less emotionally stable (in other words, more Neurotic) are heavy users of social networking, online games and online financial transactions (Correa et al. 2010; Tan and Yang 2014). Further, online platforms such as blogs and chat rooms appeal to individuals high in Neuroticism and Introversion, as they allow them to establish social interactions and recognition that their particular personality traits do not allow in the offline world (Amichai-Hamburger et al. 2002; Anolli et al. 2005).

Online communities may still be seen as a rather innovative way to interact and, thus, the opportunity to join groups where new friendships may be formed and information may be shared appeals to individuals high in Openness to New Experiences. Indeed, individuals high in this trait tend to use social media frequently (Correa et al. 2010), participate actively in Wikipedia membership (Amichai-Hamburger et al. 2008; Jadin et al. 2013) and use the internet for entertainment purposes (Tan and Yang 2014). Individuals high in Openness are by nature inquisitive and interested in following current events, including world events (Curry 2008), and older women high in Openness have been found to comment on news stories frequently (Barnes et al. forthcoming). Openness to New Experiences is also associated with a greater propensity to engage in online politics (Ha et al. 2013; Jordan et al. 2015; Quintelier and Theocharis 2013) and political discussions and activism (Russo and Amnå 2016).

Research into both Conscientiousness and Agreeableness in relation to internet usage has been largely inconclusive. Online activity and Conscientiousness has been shown to have a negative relation (Landers and Lounsbury 2006; Ryan and Xenos 2011), no relation (Guadagno et al. 2008; Ross et al. 2009) and a positive relation (Hughes et al. 2012). These inconsistencies might relate to the topic area. For example, social media would probably be considered a waste of time for individuals high in Conscientiousness, as people high in this trait consider using the internet for work and personal benefits as a diligent and effective way to stay up-to-date (Amichai-Hamburger et al. 2016). Quintelier and Theocharis (2013) found that, while individuals high in Conscientiousness were sceptical about using social media sites such as Facebook, they did not appear to avoid online engagement through other sites (for example, blogs, online forums and emails). Conversely, Russo and Amnå (2016) found that individuals high in Conscientiousness were less engaged in online activity because they spent less time on the internet overall.

No link has been demonstrated between Agreeableness and the use of the internet to get useful information (Cullen and Morse 2011) or to make online contact (Ross et al. 2009). However, individuals high in Agreeableness tend to perceive new technology as useful (Devaraj et al. 2008) and are characterised by a cooperative and forgiving nature (McElroy et al. 2007); thus, participation in an online community might be encouraged by a strong sense of cohesive community. Interestingly, blogging appears to provide individuals high in Agreeableness with an outlet for seeking favours from others and expressing concern for their welfare (Fullwood et al. 2015).

From the research outlined above, it is clear that our personalities can influence our motivations for online engagement as well as the types of activities we undertake online. However, to truly understand how personality impacts upon online commenting culture, we need explore the correlation between personality and the type and style of comments an individual will write.

TYPES OF ONLINE COMMENTS AND PERSONALITY

As outlined in the first chapter, studies that have drawn on the theoretical approach of uses and gratifications have found that individuals who leave comments are motivated by individual-centric reasons, which include seeking information, expressing a sentiment (personal-identity reasons), injecting humour or debating with others for entertainment purposes. Social interaction has also been identified as a factor in writing comments, as certain individuals want to engage with others specifically to sympathise, leave condolences or applaud good work (Diakopoulos and Naaman 2011; Springer et al. 2015). Drawing on this work, we can also connect an individual's personality to their frequency of commenting and the types of comments they make. For example, Extraverts, when engaged in online activity, are inclined to use informational comments as a platform to voice their opinions and share knowledge and information (Amiel and Sargent 2004; Quintelier and Theocharis 2013; Russo and Amnå 2016; Tuten and Bosnjak 2001). They are also likely to use entertainment comments, particularly humour, in their discussions and debates with others (Greven et al. 2008) and, since they are highly sociable, Extraverts engage in social-interaction comments to strengthen bonds with their friendship networks.

Interestingly, a study that investigated online trolling behaviours found that participants higher on Extraversion were more likely to choose trolling as their favourite activity; however, the frequency of general online commenting behaviours did not differ in relation to this trait (Buckels et al. 2014). This study also made significant correlations between trolling and personality traits outside the Big Five, most notably the "dark triad" of personality traits: narcissism, Machiavellianism and psychopathy (Buckels et al. 2014). This particular study is one of many recent studies linking excessive technology use to anti-social behaviours (Carr 2011; Juvonen and Gross 2008; Phillips et al. 2006; Rosen et al. 2013). The causal direction of these associations is yet unclear. Do anti-social people use technology more than others because it facilitates their reprehensible motives?

Some authors go further, arguing that use of internet technology actually shifts users in an anti-social direction (Carr 2011; Immordino-Yang et al. 2012; Suler 2004). This is a rather dystopian view of the online world and draws it as a negative space where we will never be able to escape aggressive, vitriolic comments and where people leaving "quality", thought-provoking comments will be discouraged from participating. However, as will be outlined later in this chapter, preliminary research indicates that particular moderating policies will appeal to individuals with certain personality traits, and specific modifications to the technological affordances of the user interfaces can also encourage participation from individuals with specific personality traits. Thus, the institutions that control the platforms on which we comment can play a role in encouraging particular individuals to comment and therefore particular comments to be made.

The internet provides a platform for self-presentation and, as there is the added potential for anonymity, some individuals feel more comfortable expressing aspects of their personality that they are not able to express offline (Bargh et al. 2002). While individuals high in Neuroticism use the internet to overcome their inherent shyness and loneliness by seeking online group membership, research on Neurotic bloggers suggests they are prone to venting and tend to focus on negative emotions (Gill et al. 2009). Thus, while they tend to use the internet to foster social interaction, highly Neurotic individuals may succumb to impulsive or aggressive remarks fostered by their greater anonymity online and the need to vent.

Individuals high in Neuroticism have also been found to use the internet to seek information and for educational purposes (Amichai-Hamburger and Ben-Artzi 2003; Tuten and Bosnjak 2001). However, they are inclined to seek novel and alternative information relating to things that may go wrong, perhaps in an attempt to balance their inherent anxieties and insecurities (Amiel and Sargent 2004). As a result, they are more inclined to write informational comments (for example, asking questions) to get better informed and gain a sense of security.

Research indicates that Openness to New Experiences is associated with multiple internet functions. For example, individuals high in Openness use the internet to stay politically engaged (Quintelier and Theocharis 2013; Russo and Amnå 2016), as a source of news (Gerber et al. 2011) and to gain new insights by tapping into the variety of information and services online (Tuten and Bosnjak 2001), including online social and media entertainment (Correa et al. 2010; Realo et al. 2011) and blogging (Guadagno et al. 2008). Research also supports a link between Openness to New Experiences and a tendency to laugh and joke with others (Greven et al. 2008). These findings suggest that individuals high in Openness to New Experiences are likely to engage in multiple types of comments, including informational comments, as a means of engaging in discussion relating to current events and political processes; entertainment comments, to ingest humour into discussions; and social-interaction comments, as a novel means of staying connected with their online social networks.

Individuals high in Agreeableness prefer to spend time on the internet to communicate with friends (Quintelier and Theocharis 2013). They are more inclined to leave social-interaction comments meant to sympathise, condole or applaud good work and, since this trait is closely associated with conflict avoidance, they are not likely to leave impulsive, aggressive comments. They will also avoid personal-identity comments expressing sentiment, as a method to avoid discussion of a negative nature. The anonymity of the online forum appeals to individuals high in Agreeableness. When their identity remains undisclosed, they are more likely than people who are low in this trait to share knowledge with others and leave informational comments asking questions about issues, in order to stay up-to-date on current events. This is because the anonymity allows them to feel they will avoid some sort of dispute (Matzler et al. 2008; Mooradian et al. 2006). Given that those who are Disagreeable have less empathy and are suspicious and unco-operative they will be more likely to be associated with anti-social or uncivil comments.

Conscientious individuals tend to use the internet to search for information and communicate with friends (Hughes et al. 2012; Russo and Amnå 2016). Conscientiousness is also positively correlated with greater knowledge-sharing (Matzler et al. 2008; Mooradian et al. 2006), which is largely driven by altruistic ideology and a sense of obligation (McLure Wasko and Faraj 2000), factors that are closely linked to the characteristic traits of Conscientiousness. However, Jadin et al. (2013) argue that while pro-social values increase the likelihood of knowledge-sharing, this is moderated by motivation, indicating that an individual high in this trait needs to have some personal incentive to share knowledge, such as benefiting from the flow of information that online commenting allows (Blumer and Döring 2012). Consequently, individuals high in Conscientiousness are likely to write informational comments that will allow them to share knowledge and information and educate others, particularly if knowledge-sharing is related to work or study. Further, they might be inclined to write social-interaction comments (for example, leaving condolences or applauding good work and personal achievements), as this relates to their dependable and disciplined nature. Those who are low in Conscientiousness, or are Disorganised, will be more likely to leave impulsive comments which could lead to anti-social behaviour.

What the research outlined suggests is that, while most individuals engage in online activity, the types of behaviours and motivations for online engagement vary significantly according to their personality traits. Extraverts are largely driven by the desire to enhance and strengthen their relationships with others, whereas Neurotic individuals seek a sense of belonging and support from others. Individuals high in Openness to Experience revel in most online activity, as it is still considered a novel way to stay in contact and gain information. Both Agreeableness and Conscientiousness correlate negatively with general internet use; however, individuals high in either of these traits do find the internet useful and may engage in online activity if there is, respectively, less chance of conflict and an opportunity for personal gain.

Understanding the correlations between personality, the motivation for online engagement and the type of comments left enables us to draw a picture of the characters that occupy comment threads. Specifically, the research suggests that individuals high in Extraversion, Neuroticism and

Disagreeableness and low in Conscientiousness are more likely to leave the sorts of comments associated with anti-social behaviour. In contrast, those who score high in Agreeableness, Openness and Conscientiousness may be prone to more pro-social behaviour.

It follows that a greater diversity in the types of individuals commenting should result in a more diverse range of the types of comments written. Therefore, online communities characterised by aggressive or vitriolic comments could be dominated by individuals with personality traits associated with those comments (for example, Extraversion, Neuroticism, Disagreeableness and Disorganised), and encouraging engagement by individuals associated with more constructive comments (for example, Agreeableness, Openness and Conscientiousness) could address this imbalance. A greater number of pro-social comments can also produce a flow-on effect for community development. Studies suggest that the tone and style of other comments can affect the propensity of an individual to engage with an online community (Springer et al. 2015; Chung and Yoo 2008).

How, then, can we encourage more engagement from the individuals associated with more constructive commenting? An understanding of the influence of personality on preference for particular moderation policies and technological affordances offers much towards addressing this question.

PERSONALITY AND INSTITUTIONAL FACTORS

As outlined in Chap. 1, the online places in which we can comment are many and varied, but, within these platforms, factors such as moderation policies and the user interfaces that we access to post comments can have a significant impact on our participatory behaviours (de Souza and Preece 2004; Reich 2011). Researchers are beginning to focus on these institutional responses to explain the degree of civility or hostility in user comments (Ksiazek 2015), and personality offers many clues as to how taking certain measures in moderating policies and modifications to user interfaces will encourage participation from particular individuals (for a summary, see Table 4.1).

Research into the role of moderation in managing the quality of discussion is particularly prolific within journalism studies, as news organisations continue to invest heavily in moderation software and staffing solutions. Moderation has been shown to influence how open and inclusive we think

Table 4.1 Personality traits and online activity

Online behaviour	Comment type	Motivation for online engagement	Implication for user interface design	Implication for moderation policies
Extraversion Uses internet more Larger networks on social media (e.g. Facebook) *Introversion:* Social network services and other services for communication such as chat rooms and text chat *Neurotic:* Extensive use of the internet including social-networking services, blogging and chat rooms	*Extraversion:* Trolling and argumentative Political comments (e.g. local event such as elections) Informational comments to voice their opinions, share knowledge and information Entertaining and humorous *Neurotic:* Interaction comments to foster a sense of belonging. Inclined to use comments as self-therapy and catharsis, including negative and venting comments Information seeking to stay informed and gain a sense of security Impulsive or aggressive remarks *Emotionally Stable:* More considered and less reactive in their comment-making	*Extraversion:* Goal-orientated and instrumental use of internet services as a means to seek, maintain and enhance offline friendships *Introversion:* An alternative to social activities or may not engage at all *Neurotic:* Gain a sense of belonging and social support To stay informed	*Extraversion:* Will prefer to be identified perhaps with user accounts connected across platforms *Introversion:* Interfaces that allow some degree of anonymity such as use of pseudonyms, or interfaces that have an option of remaining anonymous *Neurotic:* Enabling factors such as reassurance of unique contribution, receiving reward for contributing and positive feedback Interface that allow some degree of anonymity such as use of pseudonyms, or interfaces that have an option of remaining anonymous	*Extraversion:* Less strict policies More revealing communication medium *Introversion:* Highly moderated sites which would temper out negative comments and trolling behaviour *Neurotic:* Extensive use of the internet including social-networking services, blogging and chat rooms

(continued)

Table 4.1 (continued)

Online behaviours	Comment type	Motivation for online engagement	Implication for user interface design	Implication for moderation policies
Openness: Frequent use of general online activity including social media, Wikipedia, entertainment, news forums, political engagement and blogging	*Openness:* Social-interaction and humorous comments Informational comments involving current events and political processes Social-interaction comments to stay in touch with their online social network	*Openness:* Creative outlet, gain insight, set a trend and learn new online technologies Tapping into variety of information and online services *Closed:* Less likely to go to unfamiliar websites	*Openness:* Highly likely to be engaged in online commenting, particularly if the interface is modern and kept up-to-date with new technologies and current trends *Closed:* Prefer the option to personalise interfaces to suit individual taste and needs	*Openness:* Some moderation might be preferable; however, should still be able to post comments pushing the boundaries of what is considered socially acceptable
Agreeable: Negative correlation with general internet usage, including Wikipedia, email, instant messaging and information-seeking	*Agreeable:* Social-interaction comments to express sympathy, leave condolences or applaud good work Informational comments to ask questions Less likely to leave impulsive or aggressive comments or personal-identity comments *Disagreeable:* Uncivil, disruptive, argumentative comments	*Agreeable:* New technologies perceived as useful. To stay up-to-date on current events, help and seek favours from others	*Agreeable:* Less-revealing communication medium (e.g. low visibility) and choice of anonymity More likely to engage in interfaces that are user friendly, promote a strong sense of community and aid online contribution *Disagreeable:* Preference for limited self-disclosure *Disagreeable:* Due to their suspicious nature will not like anonymity	*Agreeable:* Effective moderation policies to weave out aggressive and conflict-seeking behaviour

(continued)

Table 4.1 (continued)

Online behaviours	Comment type	Motivation for online engagement	Implication for user interface design	Implication for moderation policies
Conscientious: Disciplined, diligent, dependable, detail-oriented, like to plan ahead, are thorough and are persistent *Disorganised:* Scattered, impulsive and spontaneous	*Conscientious:* Spend less time overall online Negative correlation to social media sites such as Facebook, but do use other sites such as blogs, online forums and emails	*Conscientious:* Information comments to share knowledge, seek information and educate others. Social-interaction comments *Disorganised:* Impulsive and emotional comments	*Conscientious:* Advance work performance and/or have a personal benefit (e.g. academic pursuit, information sharing) Knowledge sharing	*Conscientious:* User interface should allow for detailed comments, be work orientated and look professional Exchange and sharing of information for a clear purpose Less anonymity to reduce trolling and time-wasting comments High quality and nature of comments important *Disorganised:* Dislikes time-consuming interfaces—complex sign-up and verification process

(continued)

Costa and McCrae (1992)
Extraversion: outgoing, social, upbeat, friendly, assertive and gregarious
Introversion: quiet, low key, deliberate, reserved in social situations, reflective, preference for solitary activities
Neuroticism: anxious, insecure, sensitive to ridicule, self-conscious and vulnerable

Table 4.1 (continued)

Emotional stability: less upset and less emotionally reactive, calm, emotionally stable, free from persistent negative feelings

Open to new experiences: artistic, intellectually curious, open to emotion, adventure-seeking, imaginative and novelty-seeking

Closed-minded: conventional, traditional interests, prefer familiarity over novelty, conservative and resistant to change

Agreeable: sympathetic, trusting, co-operative, modest and straightforward

Disagreeable: less empathy, less concerned with others, suspicious, unfriendly and unco-operative

Conscientiousness: disciplined, diligent, dependable, detail-oriented, like to plan ahead, are thorough and are persistent

Disorganised: scattered, impulsive and spontaneous

an online community is and therefore can inhibit our participation (Reich 2011). Numerous studies have also shown that moderation is associated with higher levels of civility (Coe et al. 2014; Diakopoulos and Naaman 2011; Ruiz et al. 2011).

Moderation can be undertaken in multiple ways. Premoderation is the screening of comments before they appear on the site and is generally more commonly used by news websites. Postmoderation is actively reviewing or retroactively removing comments that are flagged or reported as hostile, and is the method used by social media networks such as Facebook and Twitter. However, many news organisations and specialist forums will use a combination of both practices. Involvement by members of the community in moderating comments is another method that has been shown to be beneficial. This is because it is perceived as more legitimate and thus more effective (Kiesler et al. 2012).

The specific technological affordances of the interface that we use to leave comments will also influence participation in an online community. Described as "usability", these affordances will either enhance or inhibit sociability and discussion (de Souza and Preece 2004). The design of the interface will influence how easily and quickly we communicate with each other. For example, if we need to log in each time we wish to engage, we will not be able to quickly or easily communicate with our network. The interface will also influence how we react to each other's comments; for example, Facebook offers a range of emotional reactions, while YouTube offers both thumbs-up and thumbs-down. Overall, the user interface will impact on how well we perform activities, and therefore the sense of satisfaction and belonging we gain from the online community hosted by that platform (de Souza and Preece 2004), and will ultimately play a role in establishing normative behaviours within that community (Kiesler et al. 2012). Our overall sense of belonging to an online community will influence any feelings of loyalty, which will in turn impact upon our frequency of use (Barnes 2014; Lin 2008).

Modifications to user interfaces that have been shown to impact on the levels of hostility and civility within an online discussion include introducing user registration or removing anonymity; conveying clear guidelines about acceptable behaviour; giving feedback and rewards; and implementing a reputation-management system.

While the ability to comment anonymously has been linked to more frequent commenting (Meyer and Carey 2014), a lack of anonymity has been shown to increase the civility of online discussion, as comments become connected to personally identifiable information, creating a surveillance effect (Ksiazek 2015).

If an interface clearly displays a code of conduct, it has been shown to increase pro-social behaviour (Kiesler et al. 2012). This includes highlighting or displaying examples of appropriate behaviour as well as publicly showing the consequences of inappropriate behaviour. Public recognition of appropriate behaviour through feedback can also increase pro-social behaviour. As Kiesler et al. (2012, p.146) note:

> Just as some workplaces prominently display a sign showing the number of days since the last workplace injury, a community could display the number of messages since the last reported abuse or the (low) percentage of messages flagged for violating the community's official policies.

Rewarding people who have a history of appropriate behaviour also encourages more of that behaviour (Kiesler et al. 2012). Rewards could include increasing the benefits of participation by not applying specific community rules to that individual (for example, quotas on number of contributions), or elevating the status of that individual to a community moderator.

Reputation-management systems are also effective tools for enhancing pro-social behaviours. Reputation-management systems create a "reputation economy" (Braun 2015), whereby users can rate or vote on each other's comments to incentivise pro-social behaviour. This type of interface design enables community members to police their own discussions and can be associated with a cohesive and engaged community (Ksiazek 2015). Other forms of this style of intervention include "flagging", which refers to an individual referring a comment to a professional moderator for deletion (Naab et al. 2016).

CONCLUSION: THE BIG PICTURE—PERSONALITY AND COMMENTING

Both moderation and user-interface design can radically influence online behaviour. Drawing on the research into the Big Five personality traits and online behaviour outlined above, it becomes possible to determine which moderation practices and interface designs will appeal to particular individuals. For example, Extraverts will prefer less-strict moderation policies that allow more revealing communication, and a user interface that requires them to be identified, perhaps connecting user accounts across platforms. Introverts, however, will prefer highly moderated sites, which would temper out negative comments, and an interface that allows a degree of anonymity, such as the use of pseudonyms. Highly Neurotic individuals will also prefer highly moderated sites, to ensure they will not receive negative comments; however, they will prefer an interface design that has enabling factors such as reassurance of unique contribution, rewards for contributing and positive feedback (perhaps through a reputation-management system). For people high in Openness, some moderation might be preferable; however, these individuals would still prefer to be able to post comments that push the boundaries of what is considered socially acceptable. In contrast, those less Open will prefer the option of personalising interfaces to suit their individual taste and needs. It is highly likely that people high in Openness will be engaged in online commenting if the interface is modern and kept up-to-date with new technologies and current trends. People who are Agreeable are more likely to comment where moderation is strict, to weave out aggressive and conflict-seeking behaviour. Agreeable individuals will prefer anonymity in interface design as they have a preference for limited self-disclosure. Those who are Disagreeable will be suspicious of anonymous comments, making them less likely to comment on interfaces that enable this. It is interesting to note that, while the ability to make anonymous contributions has been linked to more hostile online communities (Ksiazek 2015; Meyer and Carey 2014), removal of this option entirely could inhibit participation by not only those associated with aggressive or anti-social comments, but also those high in Agreeableness, who are associated with community-enhancing social interaction and informational comments. Agreeable individuals will also prefer interfaces that promote a strong sense of community and aid online contribution. For Conscientious individuals, high levels of moderation will be important to remove what they deem "time-wasting" comments. A reputation-management system, through which "quality" comments are rewarded and commenters can publicly rank each other's comments to encourage debate, will also appeal to Conscientious individuals. Additionally, a user interface should allow for detailed comments, be work-orientated and look professional to appeal to these individuals. Those low in Conscientiousness will be more likely to comment on user interfaces that do not offer barriers or are time-consuming, (for example, by making new members undertake a complex sign-up procedure or verification process).

While it is clear that there is a need for further research in this field, the work of psychology scholars offers much towards understanding commenting culture. It enables us to recognise the particular characters that operate in this space, their motivations for participation and their propensity for making particular types of comments. Understanding the role of personality in commenting also provides evidence that the institutions that control the landscape in which we make our comments, like Facebook and Twitter, news organisations and other hosts of online discussion, can take an active role, through interface design and moderation, in enhancing the diversity of the individuals making comments. Such intervention has the potential to impact upon the level of anti-social behaviour online.

In the next chapter, the role that the game industry, in particular game publisher Riot Games, has taken in actively combating anti-social behaviour will be outlined to examine these institutional factors more fully.

REFERENCES

Amichai-Hamburger, Yair, and Elisheva Ben-Artzi. 2003. Loneliness and Internet Use. *Computers in Human Behavior* 19 (1): 71–80.
Amichai-Hamburger, Yair, Galit Wainapel, and Shaul Fox. 2002. 'On the Internet No One Knows I'm an Introvert': Extroversion, Neuroticism, and Internet Interaction. *Cyberpsychology & Behavior* 5 (2): 125–128.
Amichai-Hamburger, Yair, Naama Lamdan, Rinat Madiel, and Tsahi Hayat. 2008. Personality Characteristics of Wikipedia Members. *CyberPsychology & Behavior* 11 (6): 679–681.
Amichai-Hamburger, Yair, Tali Gazit, Judit Bar-Ilan, Oren Perez, Noa Aharony, Jenny Bronstein, and Talia Sarah Dyne. 2016. Psychological Factors Behind the Lack of Participation in Online Discussions. *Computers in Human Behavior* 55: 268–277.
Amiel, Tel, and Stephanie Lee Sargent. 2004. Individual Differences in Internet Usage Motives. *Computers in Human Behavior* 20 (6): 711–726.
Andreassen, Cecilie Schou, Mark D. Griffiths, Siri Renate Gjertsen, Elfrid Krossbakken, Siri Kvam, and Ståle Pallesen. 2013. The Relationships Between Behavioral Addictions and the Five-Factor Model of Personality. *Journal of Behavioral Addictions* 2 (2): 90–99.
Anolli, Luigi, Daniela Villani, and Giuseppe Riva. 2005. Personality of People Using Chat: An On-Line Research. *CyberPsychology & Behavior* 8 (1): 89–95.
Bargh, John A., Katelyn Y.A. McKenna, and Grainne M. Fitzsimons. 2002. Can You See the Real Me? Activation and Expression of the 'True Self' on the Internet. *Journal of Social Issues* 58 (1): 33–48.

Barnes, Renee. 2014. The 'Ecology of Participation' a Study of Audience Engagement on Alternative Journalism Websites. *Digital Journalism* 2 (4): 542–557.

Barnes, Renee, Doug Mahar, Wendell Cockshaw, and Idee Wong. forthcoming. Personality and online news commenting behaviours: Uncovering the characteristics of those below the line. *Media International Australia.*

Blanchard, Anita L., and M. Lynne Markus. 2002. *Sense of Virtual Community-Maintaining the Experience of Belonging.* System Sciences, 2002. HICSS. Proceedings of the 35th Annual Hawaii International Conference on System Sciences, Big Island.

Blau, Ina, and Azy Barak. 2012. How Do Personality, Synchronous Media, and Discussion Topic Affect Participation? *Educational Technology & Society* 15 (2): 12–24.

Blumer, Tim, and Nicola Döring. 2012. Are We the Same Online? The Expression of the Five Factor Personality Traits on the Computer and the Internet. *Cyberpsychology: Journal of Psychosocial Research on Cyberspace* 6 (3): np.

Brandtzæg, Petter Bae. 2012. Social Networking Sites: Their Users and Social Implications—A Longitudinal Study. *Journal of Computer-Mediated Communication* 17 (4): 467–488. https://doi.org/10.1111/j.1083-6101.2012. 01580.x.

Braun, Joshua A. 2015. News Programs: Designing MSNBC. com's Online Interfaces. *Journalism* 16 (1): 27–43.

Buckels, Erin E., Paul D. Trapnell, and Delroy L. Paulhus. 2014. Trolls Just Want to Have Fun. *Personality and Individual Differences* 67: 97–102.

Carr, Nicholas. 2011. *The Shallows: What the Internet Is Doing to Our Brains.* New York: WW Norton & Company.

Chung, Deborah S., and Chan Yun Yoo. 2008. Audience Motivations for Using Interactive Features: Distinguishing Use of Different Types of Interactivity on an Online Newspaper. *Mass Communication and Society* 11 (4): 375–397.

Coe, Kevin, Kate Kenski, and Stephen A. Rains. 2014. Online and Uncivil? Patterns and Determinants of Incivility in Newspaper Website Comments. *Journal of Communication* 64 (4): 658–679.

Correa, Teresa, Amber Willard Hinsley, and Homero Gil De Zuniga. 2010. Who Interacts on the Web?: The Intersection of Users' Personality and Social Media Use. *Computers in Human Behavior* 26 (2): 247–253.

Costa, Paul T., and Robert R. McCrae. 1992. Normal Personality Assessment in Clinical Practice: The NEO Personality Inventory. *Psychological Assessment* 4 (1): 5.

Cullen, Rowena, and Sarah Morse. 2011. *Who's Contributing: Do Personality Traits Influence the Level and Type of Participation in Online Communities?* System Sciences (HICSS) 2011 44th Hawaii International Conference on System Sciences, Big Island.

Curry, Mila. 2008. *Personality and the News: The Five-Factor Model and Headline Preferences*. Florida Atlantic University.

de Souza, Clarisse Sieckenius, and Jenny Preece. 2004. A Framework for Analyzing and Understanding Online Communities. *Interacting with Computers* 16 (3): 579–610.

Devaraj, Sarv, Robert F. Easley, and J. Michael Crant. 2008. Research Note—How Does Personality Matter? Relating the Five-Factor Model to Technology Acceptance and Use. *Information Systems Research* 19 (1): 93–105.

Diakopoulos, Nicholas, and Mor Naaman. 2011. *Towards Quality Discourse in Online News Comments*. Proceedings of the ACM 2011 Conference on Computer Supported Cooperative Work. Hangzhou, China.

Fullwood, Chris, Wendy Nicholls, and Rumbidzai Makichi. 2015. We've Got Something for Everyone: How Individual Differences Predict Different Blogging Motivations. *New Media & Society* 17 (9): 1583–1600.

Gerber, Alan S., Gregory A. Huber, David Doherty, and Conor M. Dowling. 2011. The Big Five Personality Traits in the Political Arena. *Annual Review of Political Science* 14: 265–287.

Gill, Alastair J., Scott Nowson, and Jon Oberlander. 2009. *What Are They Blogging About? Personality, Topic and Motivation in Blogs*. ICWSM.

Greven, Corina, Tomas Chamorro-Premuzic, Adriane Arteche, and Adrian Furnham. 2008. A Hierarchical Integration of Dispositional Determinants of General Health in Students: The Big Five, Trait Emotional Intelligence and Humour Styles. *Personality and Individual Differences* 44 (7): 1562–1573.

Guadagno, Rosanna E., Bradley M. Okdie, and Cassie A. Eno. 2008. Who Blogs? Personality Predictors of Blogging. *Computers in Human Behavior* 24 (5): 1993–2004.

Ha, Shang E., Seokho Kim, and Hee Jo Se. 2013. Personality Traits and Political Participation: Evidence from South Korea. *Political Psychology* 34 (4): 511–532.

Hamburger, Yair Amichai, and Elisheva Ben-Artzi. 2000. The Relationship Between Extraversion and Neuroticism and the Different Uses of the Internet. *Computers in Human Behavior* 16 (4): 441–449.

Heller, Daniel, Timothy A. Judge, and David Watson. 2002. The Confounding Role of Personality and Trait Affectivity in the Relationship Between Job and Life Satisfaction. *Journal of Organizational Behavior* 23 (7): 815–835.

Hughes, David John, Moss Rowe, Mark Batey, and Andrew Lee. 2012. A Tale of Two Sites: Twitter vs. Facebook and the Personality Predictors of Social Media Usage. *Computers in Human Behavior* 28 (2): 561–569.

Immordino-Yang, Mary Helen, Joanna A. Christodoulou, and Vanessa Singh. 2012. Rest Is Not Idleness: Implications of the Brain's Default Mode for Human Development and Education. *Perspectives on Psychological Science* 7 (4): 352–364.

Jadin, Tanja, Timo Gnambs, and Bernad Batinic. 2013. Personality Traits and Knowledge Sharing in Online Communities. *Computers in Human Behavior* 29 (1): 210 216.

John, Oliver P., and Sanjay Srivastava. 1999. The Big Five Trait Taxonomy: History, Measurement, and Theoretical Perspectives. In *Handbook of Personality: Theory and Research*, ed. L.A. Persin and O.P. John, 102–138. New York: Guilford.

Jordan, Gerald, Megan Pope, Patrick Wallis, and Srividya Iyer. 2015. The Relationship Between Openness to Experience and Willingness to Engage in Online Political Participation Is Influenced by News Consumption. *Social Science Computer Review* 33 (2): 181–197.

Juvonen, Jaana, and Elisheva F. Gross. 2008. Extending the School Grounds?—Bullying Experiences in Cyberspace. *Journal of School Health* 78 (9): 496–505.

Kiesler, Sara, Robert Kraut, Paul Resnick, and Aniket Kittur. 2012. Regulating Behavior in Online Communities. In *Building Successful Online Communities: Evidence-Based Social Design*, ed. Robert Kraut and Paul Resnick, 125–178. Cambridge, MA: MIT Press.

Ksiazek, Thomas B. 2015. Civil Interactivity: How News Organizations' Commenting Policies Explain Civility and Hostility in User Comments. *Journal of Broadcasting & Electronic Media* 59 (4): 556–573.

Landers, Richard N., and John W. Lounsbury. 2006. An Investigation of Big Five and Narrow Personality Traits in Relation to Internet Usage. *Computers in Human Behavior* 22 (2): 283–293.

Lin, Hsiu-Fen. 2008. Determinants of Successful Virtual Communities: Contributions from System Characteristics and Social Factors. *Information & Management* 45 (8): 522–527.

Ling, Kimberly, Gerard Beenen, Pamela Ludford, Xiaoqing Wang, Klarissa Chang, Xin Li, Dan Cosley, Dan Frankowski, Loren Terveen, and Mamunur Rashid Al. 2005. Using Social Psychology to Motivate Contributions to Online Communities. *Journal of Computer-Mediated Communication* 10 (4). https://doi.org/10.1111/j.1083-6101.2005.tb00273.x.

Matzler, Kurt, Birgit Renzl, Julia Müller, Stephan Herting, and Todd A. Mooradian. 2008. Personality Traits and Knowledge Sharing. *Journal of Economic Psychology* 29 (3): 301–313.

McCrae, Robert R., and Paul T. Costa. 2003. *Personality in Adulthood: A Five-Factor Theory Perspective*. New York: Guilford Press.

McCrae, Robert R., and Oliver P. John. 1992. An Introduction to the Five-Factor Model and Its Applications. *Journal of Personality* 60 (2). 175–215.

McCrae, Robert R., and Antonio Terracciano. 2008. The Five-Factor Model and Its Correlates in Individuals and Cultures. In *Multilevel Analysis of Individuals and Cultures*, ed. F.J.R. van de Vijver, D.A. van Hemert, and Y.H. Poortinga, 249–283. Mahwah: Erlbaum.

McElroy, James C., Anthony R. Hendrickson, Anthony M. Townsend, and Samuel M. DeMarie. 2007. Dispositional Factors in Internet Use: Personality Versus Cognitive Style. *MIS Quarterly* 31: 809–820.

McKenna, Katelyn Y.A., and John A. Bargh. 2000. Plan 9 from Cyberspace: The Implications of the Internet for Personality and Social Psychology. *Personality and Social Psychology Review* 4 (1): 57–75.

McLure Wasko, M., and Samer Faraj. 2000. 'It Is What One Does': Why People Participate and Help Others in Electronic Communities of Practice. *The Journal of Strategic Information Systems* 9 (2): 155–173.

Meyer, Hans K., and Michael Clay Carey. 2014. In Moderation: Examining How Journalists' Attitudes Toward Online Comments Affect the Creation of Community. *Journalism Practice* 8 (2): 213–228.

Mooradian, Todd, Birgit Renzl, and Kurt Matzler. 2006. Who Trusts? Personality, Trust and Knowledge Sharing. *Management Learning* 37 (4): 523–540.

Naab, Teresa K., Anja Kalch, and Tino G.K. Meitz. 2016. Flagging Uncivil User Comments: Effects of Intervention Information, Type of Victim, and Response Comments on Bystander Behavior. *New Media & Society*. https://doi.org/10.1177/1461444816670923.

Orchard, Lisa J., and Chris Fullwood. 2010. Current Perspectives on Personality and Internet Use. *Social Science Computer Review* 28 (2): 155–169.

Phillips, James G., Sarah Butt, and Alex Blaszczynski. 2006. Personality and Self-Reported Use of Mobile Phones for Games. *CyberPsychology & Behavior* 9 (6): 753–758.

Quintelier, Ellen, and Yannis Theocharis. 2013. Online Political Engagement, Facebook, and Personality Traits. *Social Science Computer Review* 31 (3): 280–290.

Realo, Anu, Andra Siibak, and Veronika Kalmus. 2011. Motives for Internet Use and Their Relationships with Personality Traits and Socio-Demographic Factors. *Trames* 15 (4): 385–403.

Reich, Zvi. 2011. User Comments: The Transformation of Participatory Space. In *Participatory Journalism: Guarding Open Gates at Online Newspapers*, ed. Jane B. Singer, David Domingo, Ari Heinonen, Alfred Hermida, Steve Paulussen, Thorsten Quandt, Zvi Reich, and Marina Vujnovic, 96–117. West Sussex: Wiley.

Ridings, Catherine M., and David Gefen. 2004. Virtual Community Attraction: Why People Hang Out Online. *Journal of Computer-Mediated Communication* 10 (1). Retrieved December 23, 2016 from http://jcmc.indiana.edu/vol10/issue1/ridings_gefen.html.

Roberts, Brent W., and Wendy F. DelVecchio. 2000. The Rank-Order Consistency of Personality Traits from Childhood to Old Age: A Quantitative Review of Longitudinal Studies. *Psychological Bulletin* 126 (1): 3.

Rosen, Larry D., Kate Whaling, Sam Rab, L. Mark Carrier, and Nancy A. Cheever. 2013. Is Facebook Creating 'iDisorders'? The Link Between Clinical Symptoms of Psychiatric Disorders and Technology Use, Attitudes and Anxiety. *Computers in Human Behavior* 29 (3): 1243–1254

Ross, Craig, Emily S. Orr, Mia Sisic, Jaime M. Arseneault, Mary G. Simmering, and R. Robert Orr. 2009. Personality and Motivations Associated with Facebook Use. *Computers in Human Behavior* 25 (2): 578–586.

Ruiz, Carlos, David Domingo, Josep Lluís Micó, Javier Díaz-Noci, Koldo Meso, and Pere Masip. 2011. Public Sphere 2.0? The Democratic Qualities of Citizen Debates in Online Newspapers. *The International Journal of Press/Politics* 16 (4): 463–487.

Russo, Silvia, and Erik Amnå. 2016. The Personality Divide: Do Personality Traits Differentially Predict Online Political Engagement? *Social Science Computer Review* 34 (3): 259–277.

Ryan, Tracii, and Sophia Xenos. 2011. Who Uses Facebook? An Investigation into the Relationship Between the Big Five, Shyness, Narcissism, Loneliness, and Facebook Usage. *Computers in Human Behavior* 27 (5): 1658–1664.

Springer, Nina, Ines Engelmann, and Christian Pfaffinger. 2015. User Comments: Motives and Inhibitors to Write and Read. *Information, Communication & Society* 18 (7): 798–815.

Suler, John. 2004. The Online Disinhibition Effect. *Cyberpsychology & Behavior* 7 (3): 321–326.

Tan, Wee-Kheng, and Cheng-Yi Yang. 2014. Internet Applications Use and Personality. *Telematics and Informatics* 31 (1): 27–38.

Terracciano, Antonio, and Robert R. McCrae. 2006. Cross-cultural Studies of Personality Ttraits and Their Relevance to Psychiatry. *Epidemiology and Psychiatric Sciences* 15 (3): 176–184.

Tuten, Tracy L., and Michael Bosnjak. 2001. Understanding Differences in Web Usage: The Role of Need for Cognition and the Five Factor Model of Personality. *Social Behavior and Personality: An International Journal* 29 (4): 391–398.

van Dijck, José. 2009. Users Like You? Theorizing Agency in User-Generated Content. *Media, Culture & Society* 31 (1): 41–58.

Williams, John E., and Deborah L. Best. 1990. *Sex and Psyche: Gender and Self Viewed Cross-culturally.* Newbury Park: Sage.

CHAPTER 5

Lessons from #Gamergate

In 2014, there was an escalation of online harassment against women involved in gaming. In a phenomenon that came to be known as #Gamergate, female gamers, reviewers and developers were targeted by often-anonymous participants within the games, on a number of websites and through social media. Some of these attacks, as well as defences of these women, went viral and sparked intense, often vitriolic discussion.

This chapter draws on #Gamergate and the gaming industry more broadly to examine the roles that the institutions that own the platforms we comment on have in creating an inclusive and harmonious commenting culture, as well as the roles we have individually and collectively in mitigating anti-social behaviour. Specifically, the chapter will outline how some video game developers and publishers are attempting to involve their gaming communities in the active construction of safer, more open communities and the steps those who were harassed in the gaming community have taken to fight back. Finally, the chapter will examine the power of collective action to create community norms of acceptable behaviour. By examining the way in which video game developers and publishers have been attempting to respond to the problem of in-game harassment, we can explore modifications to the participatory control frameworks of discussion spaces that have the potential to create more inclusive communities. Additionally, by outlining the individual and collective actions available to us, we can create a more comprehensive understanding of the factors that affect the participatory culture of commenting.

© The Author(s) 2018
R. Barnes, *Uncovering Online Commenting Culture*,
https://doi.org/10.1007/978-3-319-70235-3_5

#GAMERGATE

In August 2014, the event known as *#Gamergate* began with the rise of the hashtag on Twitter. The event is associated with the process and aftermath of incidents in which several people engaged with the gaming community, including journalists, designers, scholars and critics, were harassed and threatened. The main targets were game designer Zoe Quinn and critic Anita Sarkeesian, as well as the people who stood up for them. The event began when an ex-boyfriend of Zoe Quinn's claimed she slept with games journalists to secure positive reviews. Quinn was subsequently subjected to a doxxing campaign (where personal details are published to incite internet antagonists to hunt the victim offline). What followed was an intense outpouring of aggression and threatening behaviour. Any gamer or journalist who publicly defended Quinn (particularly those who were female) were subject to the same abuse. Another high-profile casualty, Anita Sarkeesian, was subjected to a similar mob attack after launching a crowd-funding campaign for a series of short films examining sexist stereotypes in gaming. *#Gamergate* played out across multiple platforms—including Twitter (where the term was coined), blogs, Reddit and 4chan—and resulted in some female game developers and journalists having to leave their homes after vicious death and rape threats.

For their part, people identifying as "Gamergaters" claimed that the whole issue was a reaction to ethics in games journalism and that any harassment was and is done by individuals not affiliated with the *#Gamergate* community (despite their use of the hashtag). Gamergaters were individuals, not formally organised and having no official leader.

Overall, *#Gamergate* was a very public unveiling of the systemic harassment that had become endemic in the gaming community. It showed that, while video gamers had greatly diversified over the past decade, players who were not the stereotypical gamer (straight, white and male) were still viewed as outsiders and faced harassment because of their status (Cote 2017). It became and still is emblematic of what many saw as larger problem of misogyny within the technology industry of Silicon Valley (Mundy 2017).

Gaming and gamers, more generally, offer much to the academic study of participatory culture. Gamers are the ultimate active and interpretative audience and have often been used as an example of the benefits of participatory culture, but *#Gamergate* helps us draw attention to the darker side of online communities. As Mortensen (2016, p.13) notes:

Gamergate demonstrated how complex game culture is. It is the child of the Internet, and gamers cannot be distinguished from the users of other social media ... [Gamergate] taught us how technology designed for increased openness can be utilized to create echo chambers and to silence opposing voices.

#*Gamergate* drew focus to the participatory world of games, moving it from a "subculture" to the mainstream (Mortensen 2016). But while #*Gamergate* continues to draw out the worst from the internet (any use of the hashtag even now still draws the ire of the cybermobs), video game publishers have been at the forefront of developing innovative solutions to tackle online harassment.

GAME PUBLISHERS' INSTITUTIONAL RESPONSES TO HARASSMENT

League of Legends ("LOL"), with its 67 million players each month, is perhaps the world's most popular multi-player game and has been associated with one of the most notoriously toxic gaming communities, with high rates of abusive taunting and recidivism of those punished for harassing behaviour. This has been attributed to the fact that it matches players based on their skill level, so participants are almost always playing strangers. Other games have the ability to notify a player when a "friend", who could be someone the player knows in the real world, or a carefully vetted online friend, is online. Harassment in online gaming has been shown to be increased by the anonymity of players, a lack of immediate consequences and a competitive, emotional environment (Chisholm 2006; Fox and Tang 2014).

In response to an increase in the number of players quitting the game and citing noxious behaviour as the reason, LOL publisher Riot Games put together a Player Behaviour Team to investigate the issue. By developing behavioural profiles on tens of millions of users, the team discovered that persistently negative players were only responsible for roughly 13% of the game's bad behaviour. The other 87% was coming from players whose presence, most of the time, seemed to be inoffensive or even positive (Hudson 2014). These figures suggested that solving the problem of harassment was not a matter of banning the worst "trolls", but of adapting the shared values and norms that had been developed within the LOL community.

Table 5.1   *League of Legends* responses to toxic gaming behaviour

Principle	Create hurdles for toxic behaviour Create defaults that put up hurdles (even small ones) against online harassment	Crowdsource enforcement Use a feedback system to flag content for banning	Give clear feedback Set consistent consequences for bad behaviour (and tell offenders exactly what they did wrong)	Create norms Treat online communities like offline communities
Tactic	Riot turned off the chat function in games, but allowed players to turn it on if they wished to	*League of Legends* launched a disciplinary system called The Tribunal, in which a jury of fellow players votes on reported instances of bad behaviour	When players are banned, emails sent citing specific offence	Make *all* members accountable
Result	Before: more than 80% of chat between opponents was negative After: negative chat decreased by 30%; positive chat increased by nearly 35%	Staff audit of Tribunal decisions— agreed in 80% of cases After: regularly receives apologies	Before: recidivism high (some players actually worse after bans) After: when banned players returned, bad behaviour dropped measurably	Professional gamer Christian Rivera said of the sanctions, "It took Riot's interjection for me to realize that I could be a positive influence, not just in *League* but with everything. I started to enjoy the game more, this time not at anyone's expense"

Rivera cited in Hudson (2014)

Riot Games approached the problem using four principles: create hurdles for toxic behaviour, crowdsource enforcement, provide clear feedback to offenders and create pro-social community norms (see Table 5.1). These principles proved effective in modifying a large percentage of anti-social behaviour and in doing so provided a model for understanding the role institutions such as Facebook, Twitter and news organisations have in deterring harassers in comment threads and sometimes even reforming them.

In accordance with the first principle, creating hurdles for anti-social behaviour, the chat function in LOL was automatically turned off. Originally, this function turned on as a default in the game, so that opposing teams could chat with each other during play, but this often spiralled into abusive taunting. This "trash talk", which may vary from light-hearted teasing to malevolent insults, is often perceived as a normal part of competitive game-play (Conmy et al. 2013). Riot Games, however, turned off that chat function, but allowed players to turn it on if they wanted to. The impact was immediate. A week before the change, players reported that more than 80% of chat between opponents was negative. A week after switching the default, negative chat had decreased by more than 30%, while positive chat increased nearly 35% (Hudson 2014). Simply put, changing the technological affordances of the gaming platform to allow participants more control, and creating a simple hurdle to immediate or reactionary behaviour, resulted in less anti-social responses. If we consider relating this approach for commenting, it could simply translate into adding an additional click to the commenting process, ensuring that we actively select to engage in discussion and creating a barrier for more impulsive comments.

Next, Riot Games looked to its community to enforce pro-social behaviour. Asking the community to "flag" inappropriate behaviour is now a standard practice online. Flagging is a mechanism for reporting offensive content to administrators of platforms. Some sites, such as YouTube and Twitter, rely exclusively on these reports to trigger the review and removal of content. Others, such as Facebook and many news organisations, use flags in tandem with proactive reviewing of content.

However, flagging has been criticised for creating a technological solution that shifts the burden of problem-solving to the individual, while at the same time suggesting that this responsibility is empowering (Crawford and Gillespie 2016). Specifically, flags are determined within a narrow range of proxies for bad behaviour, leaving little room for expressing degrees of concern or even deliberating over what the community deems offensive. Indeed each individual may have a differing definition of civility (Reader 2012), meaning policing of so-called uncivil behaviour could actually result in fracturing a community. Once content is flagged, the process becomes invisible, the decision about whether the content is offensive is made, and potentially the content itself is removed with no sign that it ever existed, also removing any chance for the community to openly develop its own values and norms. Instead, a "more social mechanism for a social problem" (Crawford and Gillespie 2016, p. 421) is needed. Riot Games' answer is a disciplinary system called The Tribunal, in which a jury of fellow players votes on reported instances of bad behaviour. The Tribunal then metes out the punishment, which may be anything from email warnings to longer-term bans. The company hailed the system a success: staff auditors agreed with The Tribunal's verdict in 80% of cases (Hudson 2014). To a certain extent, this system still happens "behind closed doors"—only frequent players are eligible to participate in The Tribunal, and participation is compensated through a point structure that rewards Tribunal members for being "correct" or voting with the majority. This gives little encouragement for strong deliberation because, if an individual does not vote with the majority, he or she will get less access to the reporting process. As an alternative, Crawford and Gillespie (2016) point to the open backstage model of Wikipedia, where quality of content is openly debated and the decisions to keep or remove content are visible and preserved over time. Ultimately, Crawford and Gillespie (2016, p. 424) conclude that mechanisms like "flags may be structurally insufficient to serve platforms' obligations to public discourse, failing to contend with deeper tensions at work".

In another alternative to relying solely on flagging, Twitter, in attempt to deal with complaints of increased misogyny, piloted an approach to the governance of harassment when it granted Women, Action and the Media ("WAM") authorised reporter status. This enabled users to send reports of harassment to WAM, as opposed to using the default flagging system. Over a three-week period, WAM reviewers evaluated and discussed the reports and sometimes worked with those who reported the harassment to document a case and then escalate appropriate complaints to Twitter staff. WAM received 811 reports and decided to escalate 161. Of those 161, Twitter suspended 70 accounts, issued 18 warnings and deleted one account (Matias et al. 2015). Overall, the pilot was deemed a success as it showed that many targets of harassment needed different kinds of support in making sense of harassment. Interestingly, only 43% of the reports came from those directly targeted by harassment; the majority were made by someone else on a target's behalf or a bystander who witnessed the harassment (Matias et al. 2015). This suggests that responding to inappropriate behaviour needs a community-wide approach. Riot Games' introduction of The Tribunal, while still not completely communitarian, as well Wikipedia's and Twitter's approaches, show the importance of involving the community in developing the norms of expected behaviour.

Importantly, Riot Games looked to not only punish inappropriate behaviour, but also rehabilitate offenders. Riot Games' research showed that recidivism rates were high. In fact, some banned players were increasing their anti-social behaviours when they returned after their suspension. The solution proved to be simple: give detailed feedback via email when bad behaviour was punished. Previously, players were informed of their suspension via emails that did not explain why the punishment had been meted out. Following the changes to the email system, bad behaviour by banned players returning to the game decreased drastically (Hudson 2014). Previous research has suggested that often the source of the harassment does not intend for their actions to cause distress, or they see the behaviour as good-natured fun rather than hostile aggression (Fox and Tang 2016, p. 3). Giving clear feedback, then, is linked to the final principle—creating community norms that do not tolerate hostile or uncivil behaviour.

Central to Riot Games' reforms was the idea that their gaming community, an online community, should be treated like an offline community. If we behave inappropriately in a public place offline, we are held accountable, regardless of who we are. The same principle needs to be applied online. In what has been probably the most high-profile punishment of the Riot Games' Tribunal, professional *League of Legends* player Christian Rivera was given a one-year ban. To put this in context, professional LOL players can earn up to six figures a year, making this ban controversial and highly public. The ban followed repeated Tribunal punishments, with a harassment score placing Rivera among the 0.7% worst North American players (Hudson 2014). This high-profile ban gave a clear message to the LOL community about what was acceptable behaviour. Notably, Rivera came to represent this value:

> It took Riot's interjection for me to realize that I could be a positive influence, not just in *League* but with everything. I started to enjoy the game more, this time not at anyone's expense. (Rivera cited in Hudson 2014, n.p.)

Research outside the world of gaming supports this notion. In a study of political flaming, researchers found that if individuals saw aggression as acceptable, they were more likely to react in hostile and uncivil ways (Hutchens et al. 2015).

All of the tactics outlined above helped *League of Legends* re-define its community norms—the shared beliefs about how people are expected to behave. While Riot Games was not perfect in its execution, its methods do offer some guiding principles for the roles the institutions that own the platforms on which we comment have in deterring hostile and anti-social behaviour. Specifically, they must take the lead in proactively shaping community norms and values.

Platform owners are responsible for how the spaces in which we relate to each other are built and administered, as the technological affordances of these spaces, along with moderation and harassment policies, support specific ideas about what it means to interact in a shared space. As Massanari (2015) noted in her analysis of social news site Reddit, specific technological affordances can create a "toxic technoculture" that is fertile ground for anti-feminist and misogynistic activism. Specifically, she identifies Reddit's karma point system, its governance structure, its policies (or lack of) around offensive content, the aggregation of material across subreddits and the ease of account registration as implicitly encouraging this behaviour.

While the engagement and harassment of people who are perceived to be anti-#*Gamergate* occurred (and continues to occur) in spaces such as Twitter, one subreddit has been the public face of #*Gamergate* antagonists. The KotakuInAction subreddit serves as a hub for information on attempts to pressure companies to pull advertisements from websites that are seen in their coverage of the gaming industry to be sympathetic to social justice. Discussions on KotakuInAction also tend to be strongly anti-feminist. Without the technological affordances of Reddit that enable the organisation of this content, it could be argued that #*Gamergate* and other hostile movements would not be as organised.

It is not just technological affordances that these institutions have responsibility for, however. As the administrators of these sites, they have the ultimate power to punish bad behaviour. Indeed, workplace-harassment research confirms the important role of organisations in minimising harassment. If authority figures take victims' reports seriously and act on them, they can change the culture of harassment in the workplace (O'Leary-Kelly et al. 2009). Other researchers have found that victims are more likely to withdraw (which in a workplace equates to avoiding social interaction, missing work or leaving the organisation) if they feel that their organisation is not responding (Miner-Rubino and Cortina 2007). Equally, perpetrators will not heed anti-harassment policies if they believe the organisation will not take action (Williams et al. 1999).

Gaming scholars have shown a similar situation with women in gaming: they are less likely to withdraw if game publishers are seen to be responsive to complaints (Fox and Tang 2016; Cote 2017). Likewise, there is an onus on those who control the platforms on which we interact to ensure commenting communities are inclusive. There is still, however, a role to play for us as individuals and collectively in creating the types of spaces that we want to comment in.

How Individual Gamers Manage Harassment

Again, research into gaming provides a framework for understanding how we as individuals can help create cohesive online communities. In Cote's (2017) investigation of harassment of female gamers, she found that people who were not viewed as stereotypical gamers—white, straight and male—developed specific coping strategies to deal with negativity and harassment. In this way the women studied were "active media managers", as they developed strategies to manage the environment and harassment (Cote 2017, p. 141). The five strategies female players developed to combat harassment were leaving online gaming, avoiding playing with strangers, camouflaging their gender, deploying their skill and experience, and adopting an aggressive persona. Of course, some of these strategies have severe limitations as they hide female contributions to gaming and can become a burden for continued participation. Taking on an aggressive persona can result in a negative backlash, while leaving the game or camouflaging one's gender perpetuates the understanding of games as a male domain, which fuels the cycle of harassment. As Cote (2017, p. 149) notes, even more effective methods require a lot from female gamers:

> Just like offline society requires women to defend themselves against sexual harassment or assault by managing their dress and behavior, the onus of online harassment management is put on the victim.

In another study, women were found to withdraw from gaming entirely if they felt video game publishers were not responsive to reports of harassment (Fox and Tang 2016). This suggests that putting the onus of managing online harassment solely on the individual does not effectively deter harassment. The same study found that the broad strategy of seeking help, which comprised discussing the situation with other players and asking them for help or reporting the incident, was a more effective individual strategy for actively mitigating harassment (Fox and Tang 2016). By simply discussing the issue with other gamers, it raised awareness and dispelled myths that harassment is harmless. That in turn helped to pro-mote pro-social community values. It may also help promote bystander intervention, a form of collective action that will be discussed later in the chapter.

Digilantism is another high-profile form of individual action used to stem online harassment. While traditional vigilantes use violence to deal with their targets, digilantes use a combination of trickery, persuasion and public shaming (Byrne 2013). Digilantism is usually associated with groups like WikiLeaks and Anonymous; however, it has increasingly been used by individuals to combat cyber hate, and in particular gendered cyber hate (Jane 2016). Australian games journalist Alannah Pearce took this approach when she used Facebook to alert the mothers of under-aged boys who had been sending her rape threats on Facebook (True 2014). She then publicised her approach and their responses via her Twitter account. Her approach drew high praise in international media, perhaps, as Jane (2016) notes, acknowledging the shortage of effective strategies for combating online abuse. The approach certainly drew attention to the issue and humanised the targets of such attacks. There was also a sense of empowerment and agency in Pearce taking the issue to her attackers—one that triggered a sense of solidarity in other victims, encouraging them to come forward. However, as Jane (2016, p. 289) also notes, the over-whelming applause for Pearce's decision to handle the matter herself rein-forces a social norm that "sexualised violence against women is a problem that should be solved by individuals in private rather than public domains".

There is also some research that suggests anti-social behaviours, trolling in particular, are undertaken for publicity and to elicit an emotional response. Trolling can also be competitive, with trolls wanting to create the most emotional disturbance for their victims (Schwartz 2008; Citron 2014; Jane 2014). In other words, "don't feed the trolls", as this is what the trolls are looking for, and digilantes' tactics of public shaming could in fact encourage trolls.

Digilantism also has a potential problem in scapegoating. Mob justice can be wrong. As an example, Australian journalist Marieke Hardy was ordered to pay an undisclosed sum and publicly apologise to a man she wrongly named on Twitter as the pseudonymous author of a hate blog dedicated to her (Griffin 2011). Also, as Jane (2016) points out, there is a risk that what might seem to be fair and reasonable justice, from one point of view, will resemble unfair persecution from another. As noted earlier in this chapter, #*Gamergate* operated on this nexus, with each side insisting that the ethical and moral justification was behind their perspective. There were those who insisted that the real issue was ethics in game journalism, while others maintained that this was just an excuse for overt and destructive misogyny and the inducement of sexualised violence. #*Gamergate* has also shown that a movement can become hijacked by people who wish to do harm, taking away from the cause of those concerned by the issues.

There are benefits to individuals taking control when they are subjected to online harassment. Notably, gaming literature suggests that measures such as seeking help from others in the community and reporting incidents have the most benefit in mitigating anti-social behaviours (Fox and Tang 2016). This again suggests that creating harmonious and inclusive online communities requires a community-wide approach that involves both us, as individuals, and the institutions that control the platforms on which we comment. Likewise, digilantism approaches do have benefits such as the humanisation of targets of harassment, the empowerment of individuals and the creation of a sense of solidarity for victims of harassment, but they cannot replace the need for institutional responses to harassment. Additionally, the risks associated with this approach must be considered. As Jane (2017, p. 8) writes:

> Individuals and society as a whole may also pay a price in terms of the various risks associated with digilantism, for example, the persecution of innocents, disproportionate punishment, disillusionment with the justice system, strengthening of extrajudicial cultures online, and so on.

Instead, harnessing the collective to ensure institutional and policy responses may be a more effective form of digilantism. Similar to the approaches of feminist activists in militating against rape, domestic violence and sexual harassment in the workplace, collective activism puts pressure on the institutions that control the platforms and legislative bodies to do more to combat online harassment (Jane 2016; Citron 2014).

COLLECTIVE ACTION: A TOOL FOR COMBATING HARASSMENT

As Citron observes, the movement to delegitimise cyber harassment is in its early stages and is mostly aimed at awareness raising (Citron 2014, p. 23). The 2013 Day of Silence on Twitter, which aimed to draw attention to rape and bomb threats received by prominent British women when they suggested that Jane Austen be featured on the £10 bank note (Baker 2013), is an example of this approach, as is the numerous online petitions demanding reforms to the ways platforms handle rape threats (Jane 2016). To truly address these problems, however, an escalation of collective action is needed (Jane 2016) to push for legislative interventions or a cyber civil-rights agenda (Citron 2014). Currently, as Citron (2014, p. 23) notes:

> Civil rights laws are rarely invoked, even though cyber harassment and cyber stalking are fundamentally civil rights violations. Civil rights laws would redress and punish harms that traditional remedies do not: the denial of one's equal right to pursue life's important opportunities due to member-ship in a historically subordinated group.

Of course, collective action does not need to result in a top-down solution to online harassment. Blockbots are an example of a bottom-up approach. Blockbots are collective blocklists that are developed by volunteers and enable subscribers to stop receiving any notifications or messages from the Twitter accounts on the blocklist (Geiger 2016, p. 788):

> Functionally, blockbots work similarly to ad blockers: people can curate lists of accounts they do not wish to encounter (individually, in groups, or using algorithmic procedures), and others can subscribe to these blocklists in just a few clicks.

Blockbots emerged as an effective method for those targeted via the #*Gamergate* movement to selectively tune out content that would have otherwise potentially driven them away from the site. There were more than 3000 subscribers to one such blockbot (Geiger 2016), which enabled those targeted to refine their online experience. Geiger (2016, p. 795) has argued that blockbots "support a mode of collective action in which people are able to regain some agency over their own experiences on Twitter". However, like digilantism, there are risks associated with blockbots. Most notably, how each individual defines harassment may vary significantly, and many blockbots may be used to filter activity that could be described as incivility and not harassment as it is legally defined. There have also been instances of individuals wrongly added to blocklists, creating controversy over the role blockbots play in censorship, discrimination and gate-keeping. Geiger (2016) notes, however, that in response to this, some administrators of blocklists have created appeals boards and document the reasoning behind adding accounts to lists, ensuring an open and communal approach. Overall, Geiger (2016) argues that blockbots are a form of collective sense-making, or a method for communities to create a common understanding of what constitutes harassment, and therefore create and enact shared norms and values.

A less technical example of a collective approach is bystander invention to combat harassment. Bystander research has compiled comprehensive knowledge on what motivates onlookers to intervene in behaviour deemed to be deviant or outside social or community norms in offline settings. Intervening in these circumstances is described as helping, and the most crucial factor in an individual's choice to help is the knowledge of how to act (Banyard 2008). In an offline situation, this usually equates to an individual with medical knowledge helping during a medical incident. Online this same principle can be applied through clear community standards. Knowledge obtained from comprehensive information on community standards and intervention protocols has been shown to increase flagging (as a form of bystander intervention) from readers of inappropriate comments on news websites (Naab et al. 2016). This is because when we feel informed about community protocols in relation to anti-social behaviour, it acts as the "knowledge" required to act—just as a doctor has the knowledge required in a medical incident. Other factors that influence bystander intervention include a personal connection, so that when someone feels that deviant behaviour affects them personally, they are more likely to communicate their disapproval (Brauer and Chekroun 2005). Naab et al.'s (2016) study of news comments also found that bystander intervention was less likely if the anti-social comment was directed at a social group rather than a specific individual.

However, offline bystander research suggests that bystander intervention is more likely when the bystander has a stronger social connection to the victim (Levine and Crowther 2008; Palasinski 2012). This suggests we are more likely to intervene when harassment is targeted at an individual, or a social group that we are intimately connected to. The severity of the incident also impacts upon an individual's intention to help, with individuals witnessing cyberbullying shown to be more likely to intervene if they deem the behaviour to have escalated to an "emergency" situation (Obermaier et al. 2016). However, all of these factors are mitigated by what is termed the bystander effect.

The bystander effect is a well-established view that people help others more when they are alone than when there are other bystanders present.

This is attributed to people feeling less personal responsibility, as well as the costs of intervening outweighing the benefits (the emotional cost of non-intervention is lowered by the company of others, due to a decrease in personal responsibility). In an online context, the audiences of both a comment and a potential intervention are often anonymous and imagined (the issues of which were outlined in Chap. 3). Therefore, the available cues to establish who may be present play an important role in if, and how, we will intervene when presented with inappropriate behaviour. People observing cyberbullying have been shown to be less willing to intervene, due to feeling less responsibility to help, if there is a large number of bystanders (Obermaier et al. 2016).

However, our desire to develop a good reputation can override this bystander effect. Building on previous research, which showed that the bystander effect could be reversed if there was a salient or group identity (Fischer et al. 2011), van Bommel et al. (2012) found that a desire to manage others' impressions of us overrides the bystander effect. In other words, we will intervene so that others watching will think we are a "good" person. Using an internet forum, the study found that a high level of public self-awareness, as instigated by accountability cues, reverses the bystander effect and enhances pro-social behaviour:

> The decision of helping a person in need is based on the relative weight of costs versus benefits ... when there are many bystanders, the possible benefits of helping for reputational concerns may be much larger than when there are only a few. However, a cue may sometimes be necessary for people to become aware of the possible reputational benefits .... (van Bommel et al. 2012, p. 929)

These cues could be understood as technological affordances that make more visible the imagined audience ubiquitous with online commenting (as outlined in Chap. 3); for example, photos and personal information of other group members and a real-time indicator of those lurking in comment threads. These measures could in fact promote helping in cases of harassment. Making the norms of the community clear, particularly around the need to intervene, will also encourage individuals to be deemed "good" community members. When norms are not salient, we will adjust our behaviour to the perceived group norms as indicated by other people's behaviour (Stroud et al. 2015; Shen and Cage 2015).

Community norms can be indicated through the reactions of others to a comment (Rim and Song 2016). Naab et al. (2016) found that those reading comments on news websites were less likely to intervene if there were other comments that disagreed with the original problematic comment. This may be because such a response is perceived as a sufficient sanction and works to enact established community norms. If there were further comments that agreed with the initial "deviant" comment, however, bystanders were found to be more likely to flag the comment as the situation was escalated and there appeared the need for intervention.

Understanding why and how people will intervene when presented with inappropriate behaviour is an important component in establishing and maintaining harmonious and inclusive online communities. There is a role for us as individuals and collectively to intervene when we witness "deviant" behaviour. However, the institutions that control the platforms on which we comment also have a role to play in encouraging active community monitoring. The presence of the technological affordances necessary to establish cues that ensure we will take some responsibility for maintaining pro-social online interactions will help us to be better bystanders.

Overall, we can see that collective action is important to provide both top-down approaches (pressuring institutions and government and legal bodies to find policy- and legislation-based solutions to online anti-social behaviour) and bottom-up approaches (creating agency by refining subgroups' online experience through, for example, blockbots and bystander intervention) to mitigate against hostile online behaviour.

CONCLUSION: LESSONS FROM #*GAMERGATE*—A ROLE FOR THE INSTITUTION AND THE INDIVIDUAL

Examining #*Gamergate* in particular and the gaming industry more generally provides a useful framework for understanding both the role we as individuals have, and the roles the institutions that control the platforms on which we comment have, in creating inclusive and harmonious online communities. #*Gamergate* drew attention to the issue of gender-based harassment in gaming more generally. However, given the nature of gaming—it is highly interactive and participatory—the measures taken to combat this harassment offer many lessons in managing online participatory environments more generally.

Drawing on the principles that underpinned Riot Games' attempts to tackle the toxic culture that had developed in *League of Legends* can offer a blueprint for adapting the shared values developed within online communities. By creating hurdles for toxic behaviour, crowdsourcing enforcement, giving clear feedback to people who exhibit bad behaviour and working to create community norms that reinforce pro-social behaviour, institutions can help create a positive commenting culture.

This is not to say that there is no role for us as individuals to take in creating communities that are inclusive and safe. It is important to note that individuals have differing definitions of civility (Reader 2012), so the community must be part of the process to discuss and determine shared values and norms. While the tactics of digilantism can create further issues and reinforce the attitude that harassment is a problem to be solved at an individual level, it does invoke a sense of empowerment and solidarity in those affected by online harassment. Gaming research, however, suggests that tactics used by female gamers such as discussing harassment with other players, seeking help from other players and escalating issues to the institutions responsible for the platforms on which the harassment occurs are far more effective in militating against future anti-social behaviour.

As a collective, we have the opportunity to influence these environments by demanding top-down responses, such as policy- and legislation-based responses, to online anti-social behaviour. Collectively, we also can create agency through technological solutions such as blockbots, which help us refine our online experience.

Perhaps the most effective measure we can take collectively, however, is to intervene when we are presented with inappropriate behaviour. This is not a simple matter of ensuring we are morally accountable. As the research suggests, encouraging bystander intervention, which enhances pro-social behaviour, relies on a clear outline of intervention expectations and accountability cues being built into the interface of the platform on which we are commenting.

Overall, then, lessons learned from #*Gamergate* and the gaming industry more generally suggest that we need both institutional and individual responses to mitigate hostile online behaviour. Institutions have a role to play in not only policing bad behaviour, but also establishing shared values that encourage pro-social behaviour. Even individual responses to anti-social behaviour rely on an institutional intervention to make them effective. It is therefore imperative that we have an interplay between both us as individuals and the institutions who control the platforms to find mean-ingful solutions to online anti-social behaviour. In the next chapter, this exchange between individual and institutional responsibility will be articulated in a participatory model to understand commenting culture. Drawing on the varied research outlined in the previous chapters, it will show how the factors that affect our commenting behaviour are wide and varied, and how it is the interplay between these that creates the types of online communities in which we comment.

REFERENCES

Baker, Katie J.M. 2013. Twitter Silence. *Jezebel*, August 5. http://jezebel.com/twitter-silence-campaign-brings-out-the-worst-in-ever-1029564175. Accessed 10 May 2016.

Banyard, Victoria L. 2008. Measurement and Correlates of Prosocial Bystander Behavior: The Case of Interpersonal Violence. *Violence and Victims* 23 (1): 83–97.

Brauer, Markus, and Peggy Chekroun. 2005. The Relationship Between Perceived Violation of Social Norms and Social Control: Situational Factors Influencing the Reaction to Deviance. *Journal of Applied Social Psychology* 35 (7): 1519–1539.

Byrne, Dara N. 2013. 419 Digilantes and the Frontier of Radical Justice Online. *Radical History Review* 2013 (117): 70–82.

Chisholm, June F. 2006. Cyberspace Violence Against Girls and Adolescent Females. *Annals of the New York Academy of Sciences* 1087 (1): 74–89.

Citron, Danielle Keats. 2014. *Hate Crimes in Cyberspace*. Cambridge, MA: Harvard University Press.

Conmy, Ben, Gershon Tenenbaum, Robert Eklund, and Alysia Roehrig. 2013. Trash Talk in a Competitive Setting: Impact on Self-Efficacy and Affect. *Journal of Applied Social Psychology* 43 (5): 1002–1014.

Cote, Amanda C. 2017. 'I Can Defend Myself' Women's Strategies for Coping with Harassment While Gaming Online. *Games and Culture* 12 (2): 136–155.

Crawford, Kate, and Tarleton Gillespie. 2016. What Is a Flag For? Social Media Reporting Tools and the Vocabulary of Complaint. *New Media & Society* 18 (3): 410–428.

Fischer, Peter, Joachim I. Krueger, Tobias Greitemeyer, Claudia Vogrincic, Andreas Kastenmüller, Dieter Frey, Moritz Heene, Magdalena Wicher, and Martina Kainbacher. 2011. The Bystander Effect: A Meta-Analytic Review on Bystander Intervention in Dangerous and Non-dangerous Emergencies. *Psychological Bulletin* 137 (4): 517–537.

Fox, Jesse, and Wai Yen Tang. 2014. Sexism in Online Video Games: The Role of Conformity to Masculine Norms and Social Dominance Orientation. *Computers in Human Behavior* 33: 314–320.

———. 2016. Women's Experiences with General and Sexual Harassment in Online Video Games: Rumination, Organizational Responsiveness, Withdrawal, and Coping Strategies. *New Media & Society.* 1–18. https://doi. org/10.1177/1461444816635778.

Geiger, R. Stuart. 2016. Bot-Based Collective Blocklists in Twitter: The Counterpublic Moderation of Harassment in a Networked Public Space. *Information, Communication & Society* 19 (6): 787–803.

Griffin, Michelle. 2011. Writer Hardy Pays up in Legal Row over Wrong Online Shaming. *The Age*, December 27. http://www.theage.com.au.ezproxy.usc. edu.au:2048/technology/technology-news/writer-hardy-pays-up-in-legal-row-over-wrong-online-shaming-20111226-1pagk.html.

Hudson, Laura. 2014. Curbing Online Abuse Isn't Impossible. Here's Where We Start. *Wired* May. https://www.wired.com/2014/05/fighting-online-harassment/. Accessed 14 Jan 2016.

Hutchens, Myiah J., Vincent J. Cicchirillo, and Jay D. Hmielowski. 2015. How Could You Think That?!?!: Understanding Intentions to Engage in Political Flaming. *New Media & Society* 17 (8): 1201–1219.

Jane, Emma A. 2014. "Your a Ugly, Whorish, Slut" Understanding E-Bile. *Feminist Media Studies* 14 (4): 531–546.

———. 2016. Online Misogyny and Feminist Digilantism. *Continuum* 30 (3): 284–297.

———. 2017. Feminist Digilante Responses to a Slut-Shaming on Facebook. *Social Media & Society* 3 (2). https://doi.org/10.1177/2056305117705996.

Levine, Mark, and Simon Crowther. 2008. The Responsive Bystander: How Social Group Membership and Group Size Can Encourage as Well as Inhibit Bystander Intervention. *Journal of Personality and Social Psychology* 95 (6): 1429.

Massanari, Adrienne. 2015. #Gamergate and the Fappening: How Reddit's Algorithm, Governance, and Culture Support Toxic Technocultures. *New Media & Society.* https://doi.org/10.1177/1461444815608807.

Matias, J. Nathan, Amy Johnson, Whitney Erin Boesel, Brian Keegan, Jaclyn Friedman, and Charlie DeTar. 2015. Reporting, Reviewing, and Responding to Harassment on Twitter. http://papers.ssrn.com.ezproxy.usc.edu.au:2048/abstract=2602018.

Miner-Rubino, Kathi, and Lilia M. Cortina. 2007. Beyond Targets: Consequences of Vicarious Exposure to Misogyny at Work. *Journal of Applied Psychology* 92 (5): 1254.

Mortensen, Torill Elvira. 2016. Anger, Fear, and Games: The Long Event of #GamerGate. *Games and Culture.* 1–20. https://doi.org/10.1177/1555412016640408.

Mundy, Liza. 2017. Why Is Silicon Valley So Awful to Women? *The Atlantic*, April. https://www.theatlantic.com/magazine/archive/2017/04/why-is-silicon-valley-so-awful-to-women/517788/. Accessed 11 Sept 2017.

Naab, Teresa K., Anja Kalch, and Tino G.K. Meitz. 2016. Flagging Uncivil User Comments: Effects of Intervention Information, Type of Victim, and Response Comments on Bystander Behavior. *New Media & Society*. https://doi.org/10.1177/1461444816670923.

O'Leary-Kelly, Anne M., Lynn Bowes-Sperry, Collette Arens Bates, and Emily R. Lean. 2009. Sexual Harassment at Work: A Decade (Plus) of Progress. *Journal of Management* 35 (3): 503–536.

Obermaier, Magdalena, Nayla Fawzi, and Thomas Koch. 2016. Bystanding or Standing By? How the Number of Bystanders Affects the Intention to Intervene in Cyberbullying. *New Media & Society* 18 (8): 1491–1507.

Palasinski, Marek. 2012. The Roles of Monitoring and Cyberbystanders in Reducing Sexual Abuse. *Computers in Human Behavior* 28 (6): 2014–2022.

Reader, Bill. 2012. Free Press vs. Free Speech? The Rhetoric of "Civility" in Regard to Anonymous Online Comments. *Journalism & Mass Communication Quarterly* 89 (3): 495–513.

Rim, Hyejoon, and Doori Song. 2016. 'How Negative Becomes Less Negative': Understanding the Effects of Comment Valence and Response Sidedness in Social Media. *Journal of Communication* 66: 475–495.

Schwartz, Mattathias. 2008. The Trolls Among Us. *The New York Times Magazine*. http://www.nytimes.com/2008/08/03/magazine/03trolls-t.html.

Shen, Cuihua, and Charles Cage. 2015. Exodus to the Real World? Assessing the Impact of Offline Meetups on Community Participation and Social Capital. *New Media & Society* 17 (3): 394–414.

Stroud, Natalie Jomini, Joshua M. Scacco, Ashley Muddiman, and Alexander L. Curry. 2015. Changing Deliberative Norms on News Organizations' Facebook Sites. *Journal of Computer-Mediated Communication* 20 (2): 188–203.

True, Everett. 2014. The Gaming Journalist Who Tells on Her Internet Trolls—To Their Mothers. *The Guardian*, November 28. http://www.theguardian.com/culture/australia-culture-blog/2014/nov/28/alanah-pearce-tells-on-her-internet-trolls-to-their-mothers.

van Bommel, Marco, Jan-Willem van Prooijen, Henk Elffers, and Paul A.M. Van Lange. 2012. Be Aware to Care: Public Self-Awareness Leads to a Reversal of the Bystander Effect. *Journal of Experimental Social Psychology* 48 (4): 926–930.

Williams, Jill Hunter, Louise F. Fitzgerald, and Fritz Drasgow. 1999. The Effects of Organizational Practices on Sexual Harassment and Individual Outcomes in the Military. *Military Psychology* 11 (3): 303.

CHAPTER 6

Conclusion: A Participatory Model for Understanding Commenting Culture

In September 2017 an Australian radio broadcaster brought the issue of online abuse into sharp focus. As part of R U Ok Day?, a national mental health public awareness campaign, breakfast announcer for the national youth broadcaster Triple J, Liam Stapleton, made an emotional on-air confession about how dealing with online abuse since taking over the popular radio slot had affected his mental health:

> There's a fresh can of hate that you've gotta open up online everyday, and it definitely wears you down …. When people send things in, when people put things online, there's no repercussions of people's words or at least they feel that way. I think there's almost like a magic filter, but you know, we see it. We see when people text into our workplace, we see all the posts. We see all the comments. I can honestly say I've had nights where I've cry [sic] myself to sleep because of stuff like that. (Triple J 2017)

The segment went viral and sparked debate online and on other mainstream media about the prevalence of online abuse and what can be done about it. Online abuse does not just affect those who are in the public eye, with a recent Pew Research Center report finding that 41% of Americans had personally experienced online harassment, while 66% had witnessed it occurring (Duggan 2017). Given the prevalence and ubiquity of online abuse, it is vital that we find comprehensive ways to understand all of the mitigating factors. This book set out to uncover commenting culture—to understand what drives us to comment and make the types of comments

© The Author(s) 2018
R. Barnes, *Uncovering Online Commenting Culture*,
https://doi.org/10.1007/978-3-319-70235-3_6

that we make. Why is it that we react in certain ways sometimes and why is it that some commenting spaces become so toxic? Ultimately by answering these questions we can develop strategies to more effectively mitigate bad behaviour online.

The internet is now the place where we socialise, work and seek out entertainment, and despite the many multimedia methods of communication that it offers, text-based communication, or commenting, remains the most prevalent. It is vital, then, that we understand the factors that influence this process and how we might better manage the spaces where we are commenting. While the internet has brought new means of communication and interactivity, it is often the darker side of communication—incivility, abuse and harassment—that is synonymous with this new frontier. As Hudson (2014) remarks, "Too often, though, we talk about online abuse like we talk about bad weather: We shake our heads, shrug, and assume there's nothing we can do." But life online bleeds into life offline and vice versa. Online harassment is not just inconvenient, nor is it something we can walk away from with ease. It is behaviour that has real social, professional and economic costs. So, at the heart of this book lies the question, "How can we create harmonious and inclusive communities online?"

Typically, bad online behaviour is categorised and then equated to the anonymity and amplification available on the internet. However, we are not innately trolls, lurkers or fanboys—terms so often used to label online commenters. Our personalities might predispose us to particular behaviours that fit with these categorisations, but, as this book has outlined, there are multiple factors that influence online commenting culture.

Instead, this book has sought to draw a more comprehensive model for understanding the contributing factors to commenting culture by drawing from media and cultural studies, sociology and psychology. To begin with, it situated our online interactions within an online community. Next, fan studies, which draws from a school of traditional audience research that views media as a text interpreted by the audience, provided a method for examining the fundamental role that emotion and affect plays in guiding our commenting behaviour. Following Couldry (2004, 2014), media was then viewed as a practice to determine the interplay between our online and offline worlds. Personality, specifically the Big Five Inventory, was used to examine how individual differences influence commenting behaviour. By then drawing on the gaming industry, the role of the commercial institutions that have colonised the spaces in which we comment online was examined.

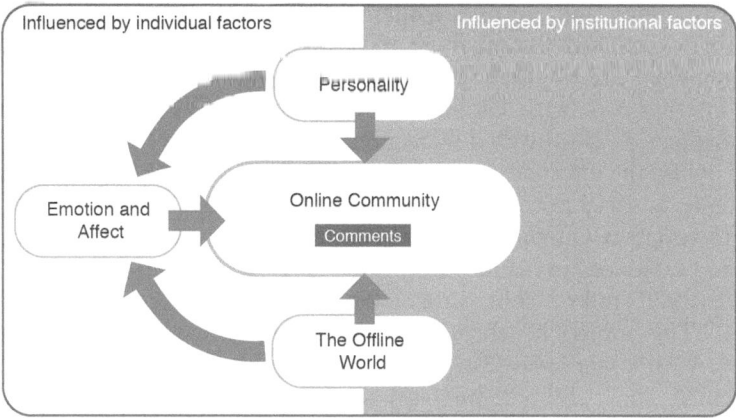

Fig. 6.1   A participatory model for commenting culture

Used together, these approaches enable a comprehensive understanding of commenting culture; how we, as individuals and collectively, can influence the online communities in which we engage; and the role that the institutions play in creating harmonious and inclusive online spaces. Taken together, the work surveyed provides a participatory model for understanding commenting culture (Fig. 6.1).

The model shows how the factors of personality, our offline world, and emotion and affect will impact upon the comments we make, which in turn will influence the values and norms of the community in which the comments are made. Our behaviour and how we respond to the behaviour of others within these communities is the biggest individual factor that contributes to the shared norms and values of a community. However, there are institutional factors of governance and technological affordances that impact upon the community, as well as influence how our offline world will impact upon our commenting behaviour, and the role of personality in community dynamics. Specifically, each element of the model can be explained in the following ways:

ONLINE COMMUNITIES

At the centre of the participatory model is community. This is an important distinction. The question of definitions is not merely semantic as what people call things will influence what they expect of them and what they are prepared to do about them.

If we understand our online interactions as taking place within a community, we can understand abuse and anti-social behaviours—those facets of online life that are driving many people away—as social problems, not just internet problems. Ultimately, online abuse is a social problem that just happens to be powered by technology. Solutions are needed that not only defuse the internet's power to amplify abuse, but also encourage crucial shifts in social norms and values within online communities.

However, as Citron (2014, p. 19) notes, when we speak up about unacceptable online behaviour, often the response is, "This is the INTERNET, folks … There are no laws here—at least not clearly defined ones." This approach—shrugging and accepting that the internet is the "Wild West", where lawlessness and incivility are the norm—is not only extremely short-sighted, but also dangerous. The internet cannot be thought of as distinct from our offline, or "real", lives. It is where we socialise, meet our partners, find jobs and so on, and we can only expect the facets of our lives that are touched by online interactions to increase. We can and must expect more from the internet, and if, theoretically, we begin by understanding our interactions online as taking part in a community, we will start to shift our expectations to line up with those that we have offline. What would our social networks, news comment threads, forums or any of the other online spaces that we interact in look like if their guidelines and the enforcement of those guidelines reflected real-life community norms?

This book draws on Keith Hampton's (2016) argument that the role that online interactions play in our lives means we must fundamentally change our conception of community by understanding it as what he terms "persistent-pervasive community". Through the affordances of digital-communication technologies, persistent contact is enabled because our relationships, and the social contexts where they are formed, are less transitory and therefore less likely to dissolve with geographical and life-stage differences. Pervasive awareness is also enabled, allowing for an easy, informal watchfulness, which provides for sustained closeness and information exchange. Understood in this way, the concept of community is far more encompassing of the role technology plays in our relationships and interactions.

An online community, then, encompasses shared forms of interactions, social ties among members, and a sense of belonging and group identification—a sense of community. This emphasis on a sense of community is also important as it incorporates people who are not actively flagging their participation by leaving a comment, but are lurking in these spaces. These lurkers, or listeners (Crawford 2009; Barnes 2016), are a vital component of any functioning online community. Not only do they make up the highest percentage of online participants (Brandtzæg 2012; van Dijck 2009; Ling et al. 2005), but also, without an awareness that there is someone listening, there is no motivation for people to leave comments. In our offline interactions, we will rarely speak if we are not heard by someone, and, online, our interactions operate in a similar way. We need those lurkers, or listeners, to be part of our community for it to continue to function.

Understanding the online platforms on which we conduct our commenting behaviour as facilitating communities is an important way to understand why we behave the way we do. Group interactions within an established community can help to establish norms that dictate how individuals are expected to behave within those groups (Kiesler et al. 2012; Honeycutt 2005; Blanchard 2004). This suggests that a strong community that clearly defines its values and normative behaviours will have stronger and more reactive bystanders, who will intervene when presented with deviant behaviour. Our need to have other people think well of us, as good community members, means that we will intervene to protect and support people who are targeted by hostility online.

The institutions that control the platforms on which we comment can help us do that. Technological affordances (for example, the display of photos and personal information of other group members and a real-time indicator of the people lurking in comment threads) can provide more concrete social cues to ensure we are aware that other community members are watching. Making the norms of the community clear, particularly around the need to intervene, will also help encourage individuals to be deemed "good" community members.

Understanding our online interactions as taking place within an online community is an important step towards grasping why and how we behave the way we do online. The community is where we direct our comments, but the mechanisms of the online community in turn impact upon the commenting behaviours that we exhibit. Contextualising our interactions as taking part within an online community also enables us to adjust our expectations, so that they are in line with the ones we have for behaviour in the "real" world.

EMOTION AND AFFECT

Often an emotional reaction is dismissed as irrelevant and irrational. One of the defining factors in the study of fans is affective engagement. However, numerous studies (Marcus et al. 2000; van Zoonen 2005; Jenkins and Shresthova 2012) have shown that emotion does not just guide the playful and creative engagement associated with fandom, but also drives more informational or politically motivated engagement. Emotion and affect can also be understood as a driver of commenting behaviour. When engaging with a comment thread, an individual may have an emotional reaction or a feeling of being caught up in the "affective practice" (Wetherell 2012) that is encouraged by the website content or other commenters. This particular "affective practice" can also inspire action, such as the leaving of a comment.

Emotion and affect are factors in binding the online community, even those who are not commenting, the listeners, to the commenting community. It can outweigh what might be a mitigating investment needed to take the action of commenting, driving us to comment despite the effort that this may take. A state of flow or a state of enjoyment while completely immersed in an activity (Csikszentmihalyi 1975) is achieved when participatory activities are informed by this emotion. This immersion can also apply to other emotional states, such as anger, fear and enjoyment. Described as "affective contagion" (Gibbs 2011), certain affects can be highly contagious and form a feedback loop. Therefore, an initial affective comment can inspire further affective contributions from others in a feedback loop. Aggression, then, can incite aggression in others, but it can also establish a behavioural norm within the community that suggests aggression is acceptable (Hutchens et al. 2015), influencing ongoing behaviours.

Our emotional and affective investment within the community and therefore the behaviours we exhibit within it will help shape the shared norms and values of that community. These are individual factors which will influence our commenting behaviour and therefore the community in which we are commenting. However, our offline world will influence the level of affective investment we make. If we have the time and are in a suitable location then our affective engagement will result in the practice of commenting.

THE OFFLINE WORLD

Just as the offline world should inform our behavioural expectations of the online world, we must also consider the role the offline world has in shaping our online behaviour. To do this, we considered media as a practice (Couldry 2004, 2014), whereby commenting is part of the larger practice of information-seeking.

Our choice of practice will be influenced by the factors of time and space. How much time can we dedicate to the activity? And where are we when we are logging on? These factors will influence whether we choose to undertake the practice of commenting or reading or choose to just check, snack, scan or monitor the comments of others. Of course, if we consider the role of affective contagion as outlined above, then it could be argued that an affective reaction may result in impulsive comments because they are written at non-optimal times and spaces, giving us less to time to appropriately consider our practice. This could be considered an individual constraint—another factor that will impact upon our commenting practice.

Individual factors such as whether we have the confidence and technical skills to present ourselves in a particular way will also impact upon the media practice we choose (Litt and Hargittai 2014; Picone 2011). These skills, of course, are socially and culturally determined. What one individual might deem appropriate writing and syntax, another may not. These skills include the ability to use the platform to make a comment, but also the ability to write or create an argument. If we do not feel that we have sufficient skills in these areas, we will not comment, because we are worried about the reactions of others.

Our ability to accurately imagine just who these "others" are, or who the audience is that will read, check, snack, scan or monitor our comments, also impacts upon our commenting practice. Just as there are those who are more attuned to social cues offline, some individuals will be better at imagining an appropriate audience for their comments online. Our frequent offline interactions will play a role in the development of our imagined audience, and that audience is most likely imagined to be "strong characters" that are "from the accessible environment" (Cooley 1902, pp. 59–60 cited in Litt 2012). This is particularly problematic given the large and diverse audience that we are actually communicating with online.

The institutions that own the platforms on which we comment can make technological affordances that will help us better imagine our audience and adapt our commenting behaviour so that it is appropriate for the actual audience. These institutions influence "how" we are undertaking our media practice, and what the constraints on this factor of our practice might be (Couldry 2014).

PERSONALITY

We are all innately different and therefore our commenting behaviour will vary according to those differences. The study of personality, in particular the Big Five Inventory (BFI) (Costa and McCrae 1992) offers much towards understanding why particular individuals behave the way they do online and can even provide insight into which individuals will undertake reactive or impulsive affective practice as outlined above.

Understanding the correlations between personality, the motivation for online engagement and the type of comments left enables us to draw a picture of the characters that occupy comment threads. Specifically, the research suggests that individuals high in Extraversion, Neuroticism and Disagreeableness and low in Conscientiousness are more likely to leave the sorts of comments associated with anti-social behaviour. In contrast, those who score high in Agreeableness, Openness and Conscientiousness may be prone to displaying more pro-social behaviour.

It follows that a greater diversity in the types of individuals commenting should result in a more diverse range of the types of comments written. Therefore, online communities characterised by aggressive comments could be dominated by individuals with personality traits associated with those comments, and encouraging engagement by individuals associated with more constructive comments could address this imbalance. The institutions that control the platforms on which we comment can help to increase this diversity by adapting and modifying user interfaces and moderation policies.

Individual differences, or our personalities, can help explain online behaviours, including the motivation for commenting and the type of comments made. Ensuring a diversity of personality types among people who are engaged in a community will help mitigate against more anti-social comments. Institutions can play a role in ensuring diversity by adapting and modifying user interfaces and moderation policies to appeal to people who will exhibit more pro-social behaviour.

BAN THE TROLLS! CREATING SAFER AND KINDER ONLINE COMMUNITIES

There has been a dangerous precedent set in the discussion of anti-social and harmful online behaviours. It is often over simplified as a technology problem—something that we are to expect or put up with if we are to continue our interactions online. But as this book has outlined, this is a limiting approach that fails to view the darker side of online interactions as a social problem that needs to be tackled as such. Because online abuse is viewed as a technology problem, often solutions are also over-simplified. Ban anonymity or just ban the trolls. Most people equate the ability to post anonymously online with enabling people to be cruel to or harass one another (Duggan 2017). This presumption suggests that we all have an inner troll and it is only that we are held accountable offline that we temper our behaviour. Of course, trying to determine just who is a troll and viewing their actions as separate from wider social and cultural factors is not only naïve, but also unhelpful. As Whitney Phillips (2015) argues in her book: *This Is Why We Can't Have Nice Things: Mapping the Relationship Between Online Trolling and Mainstream Culture,* trolling is actually the result of dominant cultural forces. Trolls, she argues, are actually a reflection of social trends in the cultural and media industries as "trolls reveal the thin and at often times non-existent line between trolling and sensationalist corporate media" as well as by putting internet technologies "to expert and highly creative use, their behaviours are often in direct (if surprising) alignment with social media marketers and other corporate interests" (Phillips 2015, p. 8). The model outlined in this book (and summarised above) also seeks to place commenting culture in a broader social context and moves away from approaches that only categorise the behaviour as having restrictive and impenetrable boundaries. Instead, it seeks to paint a picture of commenting culture that is influenced by multiple factors—a more transient process in which we as individuals will adapt our commenting behaviour based on numerous factors and the interplay between those factors.

Just because someone has behaved poorly does not mean they will always—different environments (both those created by technological affordances online and the circumstances of our physical predicament) create different socialities. Understanding commenting culture in this way moves away from the binary of "us" and "them"—where we, the average internet user, are just, fair and polite and those "trolls" or the anti-social and aggressive online users are irrational, rude and unfair. Anything that creates an "other" only incites more aggression and less responsibility for fuelling an ongoing cycle of antagonism. What the model outlined here seeks to do is address the *why*, rather than just the *what* in terms of online commenting behaviour, to provide more productive steps towards creating safer and kinder online communities. We can influence our online communities for the better and so too can the institutions that control the platforms upon which the communities form.

Taking a cohesive why-based approach that looks to the many facets that influence online commenting behaviour is important in ensuring that a mission to eradicate "bad" online behaviour does not inadvertently remove the positive as well. The internet is built on the ideal of the free flow of information, which has numerous benefits in terms of enabling important political activism and greater diversity of information. If the measures to deal with aggressive and antagonistic behaviour are too militant (removing anonymity, for instance, or limiting access and membership to communities) then you will not only lock down and perhaps eradicate the more disturbing side of commenting culture, but also the positive side-effects of online networked interactions. As outlined earlier in this book, support forums and activists rely on anonymity, for example to benefit from substantive emotional support and weed out government corruption respectively. As Phillips (2015, p. 155) puts it "attempt to smoke out the trolls ... and you simultaneously smoke out the activists". Equally though, if the internet is too open, too Wild West, with no behavioural checks then we will be more willing to accept harsh pre-emptive and punitive measures, such as overt surveillance and closed and guarded communities that could ultimately erode quality of sociality.

This is not to say that nothing should be done to tackle the problem—the trick is to, as Zittrain (2008) advocates, pre-empt the problem before we have a widespread lockdown that eradicates the positive and beneficial elements of online interaction. This is why the model outlined here should be used to advocate for a combined effort to stymie online aggression. An effort that is a collaboration between the individuals who are gathering in the online communities and the institutions that are housing them.

CONCLUSION: TOWARDS A MORE HARMONIOUS AND INCLUSIVE COMMENTING CULTURE

By bringing together work from a broad spectrum of disciplines, a more comprehensive model for understanding commenting culture can be devised. The participatory model outlined above provides an overview of the structural and agency conditions that influence our online behaviour. In doing so, it provides a method for understanding how we as individuals and collectively can influence the online communities in which we comment, as well as the responsibility held by the institutions who own the platforms we comment on.

The ubiquity of networked devices, along with the ever-increasing number of social and professional interactions that take place online, means that we cannot afford not to demand the same behavioural benchmarks of our online world as we do of the offline world. Our digital and physical lives are enmeshed and need the same consideration. As Citron (2014, p. 97) notes:

> The notion that more aggression should be tolerated in cyberspace than in real space presumes that virtual spaces are cordoned off from physical ones. But when we connect to the Internet, we do not enter a separate space. Networked interactions are embedded in real life.

This book began by addressing the unease, incivility and even abuse that now appears rife on the internet. It set out to uncover commenting culture so that we can address the question, "How can we create harmonious and inclusive communities online?"

To answer this question, we must first investigate what influences our commenting behaviour. The model outlined in this book shows that this is not a simple process, but that there are many factors that will influence if and how we comment. It also takes into account the practices of those who do not leave a marker of their engagement, but are nevertheless associated with commenting: the readers, listeners or lurkers who form a fundamental part of our online communities and influence commenting behaviours. The connection between those actively participating and those who make up the cadre of listeners, lurkers and bystanders in our online communities is a vital component of building more inclusive and harmonious online communities.

Understanding the factors that influence our commenting behaviours allows us to unpack how we as individuals can influence our commenting communities, as well as the role that institutions must take in ensuring that online communities are harmonious and inclusive. Importantly, understanding the factors that influence our own, individual behaviour can help us understand our role in creating a commenting culture. These factors can also be used to build a framework for education about online behaviour. We need the technical, written and argumentative skills to comment appropriately, but we also need to remain conscious of the disjuncture between our imagined audience and the actual audience. Parents and educators have roles to play in teaching our youngest online users these skills and how to treat others with respect, thereby ingraining productive social norms for generations to come. Disturbingly, almost 70% of those aged 18 and 29 have experienced some form of online harassment, compared with one-third of those aged 30 and older (Duggan 2017). This suggests an urgency in understanding how we as individuals can help shape our online communities.

We can all play an active role in shaping the norms and values of our online communities by demonstrating pro-social behaviour and ensuring anti-social behaviour is noted and appropriately punished. Punishment may entail a top-down measure—consequences enforced by the platform—but this will not work unless we ensure that we are part of the process. We cannot expect the platforms to effectively police behaviour if we are not an active part of the process. On a more macro level, we must advocate for legislative interventions or a cyber civil-rights agenda (Citron 2014) to tackle the more persistent and harmful online attacks.

That is not to say that we abdicate responsibility from the institutions that are profiting from our commenting. They must also play a role in tackling the social issues that have become synonymous with online commenting. User interfaces and moderation policies greatly influence the community that gathers. These technological affordances and policies also impact upon the ease with which we interact, the types of individuals who comment and even how we will behave. Importantly, if we are to learn anything from the experiments of game publishers, the institutions have an important role to play in helping the community define its shared norms and values and giving the commenters more power to reject abusive behaviour.

Social media has long faced the difficult task of balancing the desire to promote freedom of expression with the need to prevent abuse and harassment on its sites. One of social media's greatest challenges is to make platforms safe enough so users are not constantly bombarded with offen-sive content and threats yet open enough to foster discussion of complex, and sometimes controversial, topics. Social media platforms such as Twitter, Instagram and Facebook have all introduced features to help mitigate the effects of aggressive posts, such as the ability to report aggressive behaviour, options to turn off comments and block particular individuals and the cre-ation of more transparent, easy-to-understand policies for managing online abuse and aggression. But despite the countless measures adopted by social networking sites to combat harassment most users still believe they can and should be doing more (Duggan 2017). Yet at the same time research from Pew Research Center also shows Americans simultaneously want concrete solutions and safe spaces online, but they are protective of free expression (Duggan 2017). The survey of 4248 American adults found 45% believe it is more important to let people speak their minds freely online, while 53% feel that it is more important for people to feel welcome and safe online. Further showing that the issue is far from simple, the survey also found 56% of respondents believe people take offensive content online too seriously, while 43% say it is too often dismissed as "not a big deal".

The internet has afforded new possibilities for interaction, creativity and productivity, but it is not a hermetically sealed space with its own norms. Maintaining an ordered, civil and functioning society is not the sole responsibility of citizens, nor is it left solely in the hands of govern-ments and officials; it is a combination of both that provides the security and diversity of most Western democracies. We all define civility in differ-ent ways (Reader 2012). That is why managing online spaces so that they are productive, comfortable places for social gatherings needs to be done not just institutionally, but also individually. We do not all feel comfortable in a biker bar, for example, but many people do choose to go to them. There are certain social norms and community measures employed by management and the individuals that frequent such spaces that make them appealing to the particular individuals who go there. Likewise, there needs to be differing spaces online, and we all need to take an active role in creat-ing the online spaces we wish to take part in. The same can be said about specific behaviours. What people constitute to be online harassment or inappropriate behaviour is highly contextual and varies from person to person (Duggan 2017). The same Pew Research Center study found that strikingly, 28% of those whose most recent encounter involved severe types of abusive behaviour such as stalking, sexual harassment, sustained harassment or physical threats—*did not* think of their own experience as constituting "online harassment". Meanwhile, 32% of those who had only encountered "mild" behaviours such as name-calling or efforts to embarrass them *did* consider their most recent experience to be online harassment (Duggan 2017). The only way then to manage and adapt to these differing expectations is to place the burden of managing our online communities and the interactions that take place within them with both the individual and the institution.

Specifically, though, how can we manage these differing expectations? How can we create more harmonious and inclusive communities without stemming a free flow of discussion? One method would be to consider impact as a measure of antagonistic behaviour. This opens up areas of more fruitful future research where documenting and clearly defining behaviours based on their impacts can help determine structures for managing our online communities. Are the effects persistent, archived and searchable? Put simply, will the results of the anti-social commenting behaviour continue to haunt the victim. Actions that have these long-lasting impacts are those that need harsher measures, along the lines of what Citron (2014) argues for in terms of legislative measures.

That is not to say victims of one-off or fleeting antagonism are not justified in feeling affected by a negative interaction. Distinguishing based on persistence is more about ensuring a balance. Ensuring that measures to prevent these types of behaviours and more persistent behaviours will be different and we cannot determine these unless we have clearer definitions of behaviour. Situating our interactions within a community helps this process. It provides options for more community-specific interventions to deal with behaviours that do not harm a person's reputation or have long-lasting consequences. It is about maximising effectiveness without completely locking down the internet so we have no free-flowing discourse.

Regardless of how it is defined, it is generally agreed that online abuse is concerning and does not only affect those in high-profile positions, like the radio broadcaster mentioned at the beginning of this chapter. This book has attempted to move away from a one size fits all model of categorising commenting behaviour and provides a more nuanced approach to articulating commenting culture. It is hoped that the participatory model outlined in this book will be used to adjust our expectations of the online domain to mimic the expectations we have of "real life". The model is also aimed at informing individuals and institutions about how they can influence commenting culture, as well as providing a framework for media scholars to more thoroughly interrogate commenting practice.

REFERENCES

Barnes, Renee. 2016. The Ecology of Participation. In *The SAGE Handbook of Digital Journalism*, ed. Tamara Witschge, Chris Anderson, David Domingo, and Alfred Hermida, 179–191. New York: Sage.

Blanchard, Anita. 2004. Virtual Behavior Settings: An Application of Behavior Setting Theories to Virtual Communities. *Journal of Computer-Mediated Communication* 9 (2). http://jcmc.indiana.edu/vol9/issue2/blanchard.html.

Brandtzæg, Petter Bae. 2012. Social Networking Sites: Their Users and Social Implications—A Longitudinal Study. *Journal of Computer-Mediated Communication* 17 (4): 467–488. https://doi.org/10.1111/j.1083-6101.2012.01580.x.

Citron, Danielle Keats. 2014. *Hate Crimes in Cyberspace*. Cambridge, MA: Harvard University Press.

Costa, Paul T., and Robert R. McCrae. 1992. Normal Personality Assessment in Clinical Practice: The NEO Personality Inventory. *Psychological Assessment* 4 (1): 5.

Couldry, Nick. 2004. Theorising Media as Practice. *Social Semiotics* 14 (2): 115–132.

———. 2014. The Necessary Future of the Audience … And How to Research It. In *The Handbook of Media Audiences*, ed. Virginia Nightingale, 213–229. Chichester: Wiley.

Crawford, Kate. 2009. Following You: Disciplines of Listening in Social Media. *Continuum: Journal of Media & Cultural Studies* 23 (4): 525–535.

Csikszentmihalyi, Mihaly. 1975. *Beyond Boredom and Anxiety*. San Francisco: Jossey-Bass.

Duggan, Maeve. 2017. Online Harassment 2017. Pew Center Internet and Technology. http://www.pewinternet.org/2017/07/11/online-harassment-2017/. Accessed 3 Sept 2017.

Gibbs, A. 2011. Affect Theory and Audience. In *The Handbook of Media Audiences*, ed. Virginia Nightingale, 251–266. Malden: Wiley.

Hampton, Keith N. 2016. Persistent and Pervasive Community: New Communication Technologies and the Future of Community. *American Behavioral Scientist* 60 (1): 101–124.

Honeycutt, Courtenay. 2005. Hazing as a Process of Boundary Maintenance in an Online Community. *Journal of Computer-Mediated Communication* 10 (2): np.

Hudson, Laura. 2014. Curbing Online Abuse Isn't Impossible. Here's Where We Start. *Wired*, May. https://www.wired.com/2014/05/fighting-online-harassment/. Accessed 14 Jan 2016.

Hutchens, Myiah J., Vincent J. Cicchirillo, and Jay D. Hmielowski. 2015. How Could You Think That?!?: Understanding Intentions to Engage in Political Flaming. *New Media & Society* 17 (8): 1201–1219.

Jenkins, Henry, and Sangita Shresthova. 2012. Up, up, and away! The power and potential of fan activism. Transformative Works and Cultures, 10 (Special issue): np. http://dx.doi.org/10.3983/twc.2012.0435.

Kiesler, Sara, Robert Kraut, Paul Resnick, and Aniket Kittur. 2012. Regulating Behavior in Online Communities. In *Building Successful Online Communities: Evidence-Based Social Design*, ed. Robert Kraut and Paul Resnick, 125–178. Cambridge, MA: MIT Press.

Ling, Kimberly, Gerard Beenen, Pamela Ludford, Xiaoqing Wang, Klarissa Chang, Xin Li, Dan Cosley, Dan Frankowski, Loren Terveen, and Al Mamunur Rashid. 2005. Using Social Psychology to Motivate Contributions to Online Communities. *Journal of Computer-Mediated Communication* 10 (4): Article 10. https://doi.org/10.1111/j.1083-6101.2005.tb00273.x.

Litt, Eden. 2012. Knock, Knock. Who's There? The Imagined Audience. *Journal of Broadcasting & Electronic Media* 56 (3): 330–345.

Litt, Eden, and Eszter Hargittai. 2014. A Bumpy Ride on the Information Superhighway: Exploring Turbulence Inline. *Computers in Human Behavior* 36: 520–529.

Marcus, George E., W. Russell Neuman, and Michael MacKuen. 2000. *Affective Intelligence and Political Judgment*. Chicago: University of Chicago Press.

Phillips, Whitney. 2015. *This Is Why We Can't Have Nice Things: Mapping the Relationship Between Online Trolling and Mainstream Culture*. Cambridge, MA: The MIT Press. eBook Collection (EBSCOhost), EBSCOhost. Accessed 12 Sept 2017.

Picone, Ike. 2011. Produsage as a Form of Self-Publication. A Qualitative Study of Casual News Produsage. *New Review of Hypermedia and Multimedia* 17 (1): 99–120.

Reader, Bill. 2012. Free Press vs. Free Speech? The Rhetoric of 'Civility' in Regard to Anonymous Online Comments. *Journalism & Mass Communication Quarterly* 89 (3): 495–513.

Triple J 2017. Liam Opens up on R U OK? Day. http://www.abc.net.au/triplej/programs/triplej-breakfast/liam-ruok/8944112. Last Modified 14 Sept.

van Dijck, José. 2009. Users Like You? Theorizing Agency in User-Generated Content. *Media, Culture & Society* 31 (1): 41–58.

Van Zoonen, Liesbet. 2005. *Entertaining the Citizen: When Politics and Popular Culture Converge*. Lanham: Rowman & Littlefield.

Wetherell, Margaret. 2012. *Affect and Emotion: A New Social Science Understanding*. Thousand Oaks: Sage Publications.

Zittrain, Jonathan. 2008. *The Future of the Internet—And How to Stop It*. New Haven: Yale University Press.

INDEX

A

Affect, viii, 2, 17, 19, 29, 36–39, 41, 47, 93, 105, 113–115, 118, 126
Affective contagion, 39, 41, 118, 119
Affective engagement, 118
Affective investment, *see* Investment
Affective practice, 37, 38, 41, 118, 120
Aggression
  proactive, 38
  reactive, 38
Agreeableness, 68–70, 73, 74, 76–78, 85, 120
Algorithm, 18, 19, 59, 60, 62
Amazon, 3, 57
Anderson, Benedict, 11, 12
Anonymity, 9, 17, 60, 71, 72, 75, 76, 83, 85, 95, 114, 121, 122
Anonymous [website], 15
Anti-fan, viii, 39–41
Arab Spring, 54
Audience
  imagined, 55–60, 62, 106, 119, 124
  problem, 55–58, 61, 62
Audience homophily, 5

B

Babylon 5, 29
Background listeners, 7
  See also Engaged Listeners, Lurkers/
    Lurking
Behaviours
  offline, 12–13
  online, 2, 5, 7, 8, 29, 34, 41, 51, 57, 67, 70, 79, 84, 107, 108, 114, 116, 119–124
Belonging, 13, 17, 29, 70, 77, 83, 116
  See also Identity
BFI/Big Five, *see* Big Five Inventory
Big Five Inventory (BFI), viii, 67–69, 75, 84, 114, 120
Blockbots, 104, 105, 107, 108
Blogs, 3, 34, 35, 39, 73, 94, 102
Bourdieu, Pierre, 14, 32
boyd, Danah, 2, 9, 14, 55, 56, 59
Brokerage, 14
Bystander effect, the, 105, 106
Bystander intervention, 102, 105, 107, 108

© The Author(s) 2018
R. Barnes, *Uncovering Online Commenting Culture*,
https://doi.org/10.1007/978-3-319-70235-3

C
Checking, 47–53, 55, 57, 61, 119, 122
Clicking, 30, 48, 49, 97, 104
Closed-mindedness, 68, 69
Closure, 14, 18
Collaborative projects, 3
Collective action, 12, 28, 54, 93, 102–107
Commenting, vii–ix, 1–19, 27–41, 47–49, 53–55, 60–62, 67, 93, 97, 101, 106, 108, 109, 113–126
Communication
  confrontational, 4
  discursive, 4
Communities
  content, 3, 10
  fan, 7, 12, 27–29, 31, 32
  imagined, 11, 32
  online, viii, 1, 2, 6, 7, 10–13, 15–19, 28, 29, 31, 32, 35, 37, 41, 51, 57, 69–74, 78, 83, 85, 94, 99, 101, 103, 107–109, 114–118, 120, 121, 123, 124, 126
  persistent-pervasive, 13, 116
  sense of, 13, 31, 32, 85, 116
  virtual, 1, 10–12, 28, 30, 47, 83
Concertive control, 15, 16, 33
Conscientiousness, 67–86, 120
Constraints
  individual, 47, 49, 54, 55, 60–62, 119
  institutional, 60
Consumers, 5, 27
Consumption, 28, 29, 32, 35, 37, 40, 41, 70
Context collapse, 55, 60
Convergence, 28
Couldry, Nick, 16, 47, 48, 51, 52, 60, 114, 119, 120
Creative production, 29–31, 36, 41

Cross-cutting discussion, 4, 6
Curation, 16, 18, 60

D
Deliberation, 3, 4, 98
Digilantism, 102–104, 108
Disagreeableness, 68, 78, 120
Disorganised, 68, 69, 77, 78
Doxxing, 94

E
Emotion, viii, 19, 29, 30, 36–38, 41, 75, 114, 115, 118
Emotional stability, 68, 82
Engaged listeners, 7, 12, 13, 32, 50
  See also Background listeners; Lurkers/Lurking
Engagement, viii, 4, 11, 27, 28, 30, 33, 35–38, 41, 47, 67, 70, 73, 74, 77–79, 100, 118, 120, 123
Ethics, 94, 103
Expression, 3, 6, 10, 33, 124, 125
Extraversion, 68, 72, 75, 77–79, 81, 120

F
Facebook, 4, 9, 10, 12, 49–51, 56, 57, 59, 72, 73, 79, 83, 86, 96, 97, 102, 125
Fan communities, *see* Communities
Fans/fandom, 7, 27–37, 39–41, 59, 118
Fan studies, viii, 19, 27–31, 40, 41, 47, 114
Five Factor Model, *see* Big Five Inventory
Flagging, 7, 84, 97, 98, 105, 117
Flaming, 7, 8, 99
Flickr, 3

Flow, 14, 35, 36, 40, 52, 77, 118,
     122, 126
4chan, 94

G
Gamergate, 93–109
Games/gaming, ix, 16, 86, 93–97,
     99–101, 103, 107, 108, 114, 124
Gender, 68, 71, 72, 101, 102
Gibbs, Anne, 37, 38, 118
Gray, Jonathan, 29, 31, 32, 35, 39, 40

H
Habermas, Jürgen, 4, 34
Hampton, Keith, 7, 10, 13, 18,
     53–55, 57, 59, 61, 116
Harassment, viii, 1, 7, 8, 93–108, 113,
     114, 124–126
Hardy, Marieke, 102
Hills, Matt, 32, 36, 37

I
Identity
  belonging and, 31–34
  collective, 31–34, 41
  construction of, 31, 36, 41
Imagined audience, *see* Audience
Imagined communities, 11
Information-seeking, 48, 49, 119
Institutional factors, 16, 19, 52, 53,
     67, 78–84, 86, 115
Interaction, vii, viii, 1–3, 5–15, 17–19,
     28, 32–34, 36, 47, 52, 53, 55,
     56, 58, 59, 61, 62, 69, 70,
     72–75, 85, 100, 107, 114, 116,
     117, 119, 121–123, 125, 126
Interface, 16–19, 52, 53, 60, 61, 67,
     75, 78, 79, 83–86, 108, 120, 124
Introversion, 68, 73, 81

Investement, 13, 16, 19, 28, 29,
     36–41, 49–51, 118

J
Jane, Emma, 40, 102–104
Jenkins, Henry, 27–30, 37, 118

L
League of Legends (LOL), 95, 96, 99,
     108
Likes, 10
Liking, 7, 9, 48, 49
LinkedIn, 72
Linking, 48, 49, 51, 75
Listeners, 7, 13, 117, 118, 123
     See also Background listeners/
          Engaged listeners
Listening, 7, 30, 32, 41, 48, 117
Litt, Eden, 12, 54–56, 58–60, 119
Lurkers/lurking, 6, 7, 12, 13, 29–32,
     41, 54, 106, 114, 117, 123

M
Metamodernity, 13
Misogyny, 94, 98, 103
Moderation, 17–19, 78, 83–86
  policies, 16–18, 67, 78, 79, 84,
     100, 120, 124
Monitoring, 48–50, 52, 57–59, 61,
     107
Motivation, 2, 6, 7, 29, 58, 60, 61,
     70, 71, 74, 77, 79, 86, 117, 120

N
Neuroticism, 68, 70, 72, 73, 75–78,
     120
News, vii, 3–6, 10, 17, 30, 32, 33, 35,
     38–40, 47–49, 55, 59, 60, 70,

News (*cont.*)
  71, 73, 76, 78, 83, 86, 96, 97,
  100, 105, 107, 116
Non-fan, *see* Anti-fan
Normative behaviour, *see* Behaviours;
  Norms
Norms, 15–17, 19, 34, 51, 58, 60, 93,
  95–100, 105–108, 115–118, 124,
  125

O
Offline, online, 47–62
Openness to New Experiences, 68–70,
  73, 76, 77

P
Papacharissi, Zizi, 6, 7, 34, 54
Paratexts, 39, 40
Participatory behaviour, *see* Behaviour
Participatory culture, viii, 13, 27, 28,
  31, 35, 40, 69, 93, 94
Pearce, Alannah, 102
Performance, 6, 31, 33, 34, 39, 55,
  62, 71
Persistent contact, 13, 53, 54, 61, 62,
  116
Personality, viii, 62, 67, 114, 115, 120
Pervasive awareness, 13, 53, 54, 61,
  116
Plato, 67
Playfulness, 35, 68
  philosophy of, 34, 41
Pleasure and play, 29, 34–36
Political activism, 9, 122
Power, 28, 93, 100, 116, 124
Practices
  offline, 40
  online, 48, 97
Practice theory, viii, 48
Privacy settings, 59, 62
Producers, 6, 27–30

Q
Quinn, Zoe, 94

R
Reading, 4, 7, 10, 12, 29, 31, 35,
  41, 48–50, 52, 56, 57, 61, 107,
  119
Recommending, 48, 49
Reddit, 94, 100
Reputation economy, 84
Reputation-management system,
  83–85
Rewards, 18, 38, 83–85, 98
Rheingold, Howard, 1, 11
Riot Games, 86, 95–99, 108
Rivera, Christian, 96, 99

S
Sandvoss, Cornel, 33, 40, 41
Sarkeesian, Anita, 94
Searching, 48, 71
Self
  creation of, 5
  performance of, 6, 30, 41
Sharing, 11, 14, 15, 29–31, 48, 49,
  54, 56, 71
Simpsons, The, 39
Snacking, 48–50, 52, 53, 55, 57, 61,
  119
Social capital
  bonding, 14, 15, 51
  bridging, 14, 15, 51
Social media, vii, 2, 3, 5, 8, 9, 13, 16,
  28, 30, 33, 36, 39, 47, 51–55,
  61, 69, 72, 73, 79, 80, 83, 93,
  95, 121, 124, 125
Social networking sites, 2, 3, 9, 10,
  12, 14, 33, 53, 54, 125
Spiral of reinforcement, 5
Spiral of silence, 4, 54
Spreadability, 29

T
Textual poaching, 27, 29
Thumbs-up/thumbs-down, 57, 83
Ties
  latent, 9, 10, 12, 18, 55
  phantasmal, 56
  professional, 56
  strong, 10, 14, 51
  weak, 9, 10, 12, 14, 51
Tribunal, The, 97–99
Trolls/trolling, 1, 7, 8, 12, 36, 75, 95,
  102, 114, 121, 122
Twitter, 4, 12, 49, 50, 56, 59, 60, 72,
  83, 86, 94, 96–98, 100,
  102–104, 125

U
User interface, *see* Interface
Uses and gratification, 6, 74

V
Van Dijck, José, 54, 71, 117
Viewing, 6, 7, 33, 48, 121
Viewing position, 40, 41
Virtual world, 3
Voting, 48, 49, 98

W
Watching, 27, 30, 39, 47, 48, 106,
  117
Web 2.0, 3
WikiLeaks, 102
Wikipedia, 3, 17, 70, 73, 80, 98
Women, Action and the Media
  (WAM), 98

Y
YouTube, 3, 57, 83, 97